Countdown to the Principalship

A Resource Guide for Beginning Principals

Anne O'Rourke
Jackie Provenzano
Tom Bellamy
Karen Ballek

EYE ON EDUCATION

6 DEPOT WAY WEST, SUITE 106

LARCHMONT, NY 10538

(914) 833–0551

(914) 833–0761 fax

www.eyeoneducation.com

For information about permission to reproduce selections from this book, write: Eye On Education, Permissions Dept., Suite 106, 6 Depot Way West, Larchmont, NY 10538.

Library of Congress Cataloging-in-Publication Data

Countdown to the principalship : resource guide for beginning principals / Anne O'Rourke ... [et al.].

       p. cm.

    ISBN 1-59667-031-2

    1. First year school principals—United States. 2. School management and organization—United States. I. O'Rourke, Anne.

LB2831.92.C68 2006

371.2'012—dc22

                           2006030458

10 9 8 7 6 5 4 3 2 1

Editorial and production services provided by
Richard H. Adin Freelance Editorial Services
52 Oakwood Blvd., Poughkeepsie, NY 12603-4112
(845-471-3566)

Also Available from EYE ON EDUCATION

Smart, Fast, Efficient:
The New Principals' Guide to Success
Leanna Stohr Isaacson

What Great Principals Do *Differently*:
15 Things That Matter Most
Todd Whitaker

What Successful Principals Do!
169 Tips for Principals
Franzy Fleck

The Instructional Leader's Guide
to Informal Classroom Observations
Sally J. Zepeda

BRAVO Principal!
Sandra Harris

The Administrator's Guide
to School Community Relations, Second Edition
George E. Pawlas

School Leader Internship: Developing, Monitoring, and Evaluating
Your Leadership Experience, 2nd Ed.
Martin, Wright, Danzig, Flanary, and Brown

Talk It Out!
The Educator's Guide to Successful Difficult Conversations
Barbara E. Sanderson

Lead with Me:
A Principal's Guide to Teacher Leadership
Gayle Moller and Anita Pankake

Dealing with Difficult Teachers, Second Edition
Todd Whitaker

Dealing with Difficult Parents
(And with Parents in Difficult Situations)
Todd Whitaker and Douglas Fiore

Creating the High Schools of Our Choice
Tim Westerberg

Improving Your School One Week at a Time:
Building the Foundation for Professional Teaching and Learning
Jeffrey Zoul

Lead Me – I Dare You!
Managing Resistance to Change
Sherrel Bergmann and Judith Brough

Elevating Student Voice:
How To Enhance Participation, Citizenship, and Leadership
Nelson Beaudoin

Stepping Outside Your Comfort Zone:
Lessons for School Leaders
Nelson Beaudoin

What Great Teachers Do *Differently*:
14 Things That Matter Most
Todd Whitaker

Motivating & Inspiring Teachers
The Educational Leader's Guide for Building Staff Morale
Todd Whitaker, Beth Whitaker, and Dale Lumpa

The Principal as Instructional Leader:
A Handbook for Supervisors
Sally J. Zepeda

Instructional Leadership for School Improvement
Sally J. Zepeda

Data Analysis for Continuous School Improvement
Victoria L. Bernhardt

Handbook on Teacher Evaluation:
Assessing and Improving Performance
James Stronge & Pamela Tucker

Supervision Across the Content Areas
Sally J. Zepeda and R. Stewart Mayers

Transforming School Leadership with ISLLC and ELCC
Neil J. Shipman, J. Allen Queen, and Henry A. Peel

Acknowledgments

**Every encounter each of us has with another human being
either encourages us or discourages us about life.**

Gary West

Each of us has been very fortunate to have friends, family, colleagues, and mentors who have "encouraged us about life" throughout our lives. By their teachings, advisement, cheerleading, handholding, friendship, and, most of all, by their example, they have contributed to our competence and to our confidence as educational leaders. For this, we all want to express our deepest appreciation.

Anne wishes to first acknowledge her 10 brothers and sisters: Bob, Linda, Rosemary, Mike, Sue, Dick, Carole, Cathy, Bill, and Patricia, who helped her learn at a very early age the power, indeed the necessity and joy, of cooperation and collaboration. She also wants to thank two important mentors in her life: Gary West, a life coach grounded in wisdom and integrity, and Grant Wiggins, a brilliant and unselfish teacher and master of feedback. Finally, she lovingly dedicates this work to the memory of her life partner and work partner, Bill O'Rourke, who continues to be her hero and the wings beneath her wings on a daily basis.

Jackie acknowledges her parents, Jack and Marge Dunlap, who lived lives that honored others and, in so doing, taught her and her four sisters that all people have value, even each of them; Dr. Vera Dawson, her colleague, mentor, role model, partner, and friend, from whom she continues to learn and with whom she celebrates the professional and personal benchmarks and transitions in each of their lives. Finally, to her center, her best friend, and the love of her life, her husband, Michael, and their sons, Freddie and Tony, the fine men who light up their lives with energy, persistent support, questions that challenge their thinking, and love that grounds them in what is most important.

Tom shares that ideas grow in good company. The Framework for School Leadership Accomplishments that provides the structure of this book took shape in work with school leaders and with the support of many colleagues, including Gerald Ott, Cindy Harrison, and May Lowry, and the writing group who joined him in linking these experiences to professional literature, including Rodney Muth, Michael Murphy, and Connie Fulmer. His deepest gratitude to all of them.

Karen is grateful to her family for their many gifts of wisdom and joy around the family kitchen table, memories that keep her grounded in what is most important in life. She thanks two important teachers in her life: her husband, and best friend, Bill Morse, and the strong young woman who is her step-daughter, Jenne Morse, for contributing immeasurably to her growth, learning, and happiness. Finally, she expresses a loving thank you to her mother, Nina Ballek, who provided significant encouragement in life and whose memory encourages her still.

Together we want to thank all of the school leaders who participated in the *New School Leadership Project*, as well as Blaine Peterson, Linda Mooney, Mary Ellen Burciago, Dick Amman, Dorothy Buksar, and Ruth Taravella, who served as expert guides in the project. A special thanks to Rose Ena Gonzalez and Elyse Dunckley for always making us look better and sound smarter than we ever were, and to Vince Puzick, an extraordinary teacher and leader in his own right, for his assistance in the final editing of this book.

Indeed, you all have enriched our lives and caused us to feel encouraged about the futures of our children, our schools, and our world.

Preface

"Five hundred twenty-five thousand six hundred minutes, how do you measure a year in the life"…of school principals during their first year on the job? Borrowing from popular lyrics from the song *Seasons of Love*, from the Broadway musical *Rent* (Larson, 1996), the authors of this book believe that each of the seasons, indeed each of the minutes, during that "rookie year" is both memorable and measurable; measurable by the successes and, yes, by the failures; by the laughter and by the gut-wrenching, internal dialogues; by the confidence-building experiences; and by the repeated rounds of second-guessing and replaying of conversations and decisions.

The first year as a school principal is often a particularly lonely and isolating experience in which one is constantly searching for guidance, support, validation, and possibly even "divine intervention." The lucky ones have a highly successful and committed coach or mentor to serve as a listener, sounding board, and guide on the side. In our experience, those lucky ones are few and far between. The majority of first-year principals are flying solo for most of the journey and hoping that their takeoffs and landings are all safe ones, albeit rocky and turbulent at times.

Over the past four years, the authors, drawing significantly from their experiences as elementary, middle school, and high school principals, as well as professors in university principal preparation programs, have had the honor of working with prospective, beginning, and experienced principals through a grant from the U.S. Department of Education. The *New School Leadership Project* was designed to provide on-the-job training and yearlong coaching services, as well as to conduct in-depth interviews with experienced principals to gain insight into "a year in the life" of principals working in today's demanding, high-accountability environments. From our many observations and conversations, these educational leaders have taught us well. They have been very open and very direct in what they needed and what they needed to know. If we were to summarize those needs, we believe that they could be concisely stated in this four-prong "wish list."

As prospective and beginning school principals, we wish for … we need ….

As experienced principals, we wished for … we needed ….

♦ A conceptual framework, or mental model, to support and focus our understanding of the complex and intricate responsibilities of the school leader

- Structures and processes for planning, organizing, recording, and monitoring the multitude of tasks that reflect the daily life of the principal

- "Real" samples, models, and templates of letters, agendas, interview questions, and much more that appear in every experienced principals' computer hard drive and file drawer but are only wishful thinking for the novice, and, finally,

- The wisdom that comes only from the reflective experience and insight of successful leaders serving in a range of diverse organizations and settings.

Countdown to the Principalship: A Resource Guide for Beginning Principals, began as a resource for the principals participating in the New School Leadership Project and the fine coaches who served and supported them. Through its refinement and use over several years, more and more principals outside of the project requested copies, and, ultimately, we were encouraged to seek publication in order to increase its availability throughout the country. It is indeed our privilege and honor to do so.

There is no profession that any of us holds with greater respect and appreciation than that of the school principal. We're often reminded, when working with principals, of a letter that Roland Barth (1990), who was an elementary school principal and later the founder of the Harvard Principals' Center, wrote to his colleagues after taking a year's leave of absence from the principalship and having that rare and enviable time to reflect. In his letter, he used this analogy to describe the life in schools:

> A tennis shoe in a laundry dryer. Probably no image captures so fully the life of an adult working in an elementary, middle, or senior high school. For educators, much of the time is turbulent, heated, confused, disoriented, congested, and full of recurring bumps.

Having been able to readily identify with feeling like "Chuck Taylor Converse Hi-Top tennis shoes" in a laundry dryer for decades, it is with great hope that, through this book, we are able to turn down the heat and limit the rotations for the many promising principals who are just beginning their careers. We wish you good luck and good cheer in your leadership; your work could not be more important.

Table of Contents

Free Downloads

This book displays 35 Templates, each of which provides assistance to principals as they plan, organize, record, and monitor the tasks they carry out throughout the year.

If you have purchased this book, Eye On Education grants permission for you to download the Templates from our web site. They can be opened in Microsoft Word© and in Adobe Acrobat. Further permission has been granted to those who have purchased this book to modify and customize these Templates so they can fit the specific needs and context of your school.

You can access the free downloads by going to Eye On Education's web site: www.eyeoneducation.com. Click on FREE Downloads or use our Search Engine to find this book. Scroll down to find the link to the free downloads.

Bookbuyer access code: **COUNT-7031-1**

List of Downloadable Templates on Our Website

1

The Framework for School Leadership Accomplishments

Congratulations! You are now a *principal*! You have the opportunity to provide leadership for your own school! Staff, parents, students, your school community, and your district believe that *you* have what it takes to move this school forward. It is a good thing that you are equal to the task because you are already *6 months behind*!

Not to worry…You have a sound foundational knowledge base. You have worked diligently to build your skills tool box. You are learning more each day about your new school community. Now it is time to apply the important information you have learned. This Resource Guide contains tools that you can quickly use to help you prioritize and address essential work that you need to do.

How this Resource Guide Is Organized to Help New Principals

This book is designed to help new principals during the important period between appointment to the position and the first weeks of school. Most new principals come to their positions with a well-developed vision of what a school should be like. Years of experience as a teacher and teacher leader typically have helped new principals frame clear goals toward which they want to lead their schools and core values that they hope will guide their actions. They also know that first impressions are powerful, and that the plans made before their first year as principal can have long-lasting consequences.

Reality strikes quickly for new principals. Most are immediately immersed in literally hundreds of practical details to make sure that they and their schools are ready for the launch of a new year. Even for those fortunate principals who are named to their positions with a few months to plan, this is a very busy time with little room for reflection about vision and values. *Countdown to the Principalship* is intended to help during this critical period by combining practical advice with a conceptual model that links daily details with larger goals.

This chapter provides two tools for using the book. First, we introduce you to the *Framework for School Leadership Accomplishments* to help you organize your thinking about your work as a school principal. Second, we provide a template to assist you in creating your personal *Entry Plan*.

Chapters 2 through 10 address important tasks for principals and contain ready-to-use ideas and examples for your use. Each chapter highlights one *accomplishment area* from the *Framework for School Leadership Accomplishments* and describes the work of the principal related to that area for start-up and the first weeks of the school year. Free downloads for all of these examples are available at www.eyeoneducation.com for your use. You are encouraged to modify any example to meet your specific needs. Each example gives you a place to start.

The Framework for School Leadership Accomplishments

In this book we use the *Framework for School Leadership Accomplishments* (FSLA) (Bellamy, 1999; Bellamy, Fulmer, Murphy, & Muth, 2006; 2007) as a way of organizing ideas and resources for new principals. In essence, this model asks *What must get accomplished?* through the school's daily activities in order to achieve the school's larger goals and purposes.

Although every school is different, there are common challenges that all schools must face in order to support student learning and reach other goals. One way or another, every school creates a climate for students and staff, a curriculum that is experienced by students, a pattern of resource allocations that support daily operations, and so on. *Accomplishments* are what result when schools address these common challenges; they are the conditions, structures, and intermediate results through which the school supports the work of teachers and students.

The figure on page 4 illustrates the FSLA. The figure begins at the center, with student learning as the primary outcome expected of schools. Nine accomplishments surround this center, and they are arranged in two tiers to show that they influence student learning by stimulating effort of different members of the school community.

The accomplishments in the learning environment—learning goals defined, instruction provided, student climate sustained, and related services provided—all influence student learning when they affect the level and focus of student effort.

The second tier involves accomplishments that influence the effort of teachers and other staff, whose work, in turn, creates the learning environment. The accomplishments here are more organizational—resources mobilized, school operations supported, staff supported, and school renewal sustained.

The ninth accomplishment, family–community partnerships sustained, supports both the environment for teaching and the environment for learning. The school's work in this area affects student effort when it stimulates family support for student work at home, and it enhances professional effort when it stimulates family involvement in the school.

The open space to the right of the figure symbolizes the many factors outside the control of schools that affect student and professional effort. To the left, the figure could be expanded to include the district, school board, state legislature, and other institutions that affect how principals lead their schools.

Appendix A provides an overview of the FSLA, defines each of the accomplishments, and describes success criteria that apply to each (for example, all schools have some kind of climate that their students experience; what makes a climate good?). Additional resources are available for those wanting a more in-depth discussion. The research associated with each of the nine accomplishments is reviewed in Bellamy, Fulmer, Murphy, & Muth (2006), and a comprehensive discussion of leadership strategies associated with the FSLA is available in Bellamy, Fulmer, Murphy, & Muth (2007).

By identifying and organizing the accomplishments, or school conditions, through which school leaders seek to achieve student learning, the *Framework for School Leadership Accomplishments* helps a principal plan comprehensively for school success. The FSLA is a practical model that helps school leaders organize their thinking, diagnose individual schools' needs, and prioritize their work in a timely way to maximize results in student learning. The FSLA takes the very complex work of schools and organizes it in a way that is applicable, relevant, and useful. Complex work can seem overwhelming if it is not organized in ways that allow us to "wrap our minds" around it.

It is important to mention what is not covered in a resource guide organized around the FSLA. Some issues must be addressed and incorporated into your behavior consistently throughout the year: effective time management practices, effective communication strategies, including excellent written work and grammar usage, and maintenance of confidentiality in your work. This guide weaves references and strategies related to those important issues throughout the book, but it makes no attempt to recreate the good work that is already in print in these areas. Helpful references and resources in these topic areas typically are available through districts and professional libraries.

The Framework for School Leadership Accomplishments

From *The Whole School Framework: A Design for Learning,* by T. Bellamy, 1999, Oxford, OH: National Staff Development Council. Copyright 1997 by G. T. Bellamy. Adapted with permission.

Creating Your Personal Entry Plan

As you read through the *Framework for School Leadership Accomplishments,* the number of tasks associated with each accomplishment area may seem overwhelming. Many successful principals use an Entry Plan as an organizational tool when entering a new position. We invite you to begin your use of this guide by following the suggested process outlined below for creating an Entry Plan as the new principal of your school.

Following your appointment as principal, it is important to carefully and thoughtfully prepare a *plan of entry* into the school and school community. Beginning principals and principals new to a school have many entry tasks in common, regardless of the school they are entering. However, each principal must consider some entry tasks that are specific to the unique school that she/he is entering. For example:

- Some high schools have alumni associations that are active and are political forces in the school and school community. A principal at one of these schools *must* include a meeting with the officers of the alumni association early in her/his tenure at the school. To overlook investing time with this group would likely set up negative dynamics that the principal would have to invest much energy over time to mitigate.

- Many, but not all, elementary schools have before-school and after-school day care programs for their students. The schools that do so require work during the summer to support and sustain those programs.

An **Entry Planner** (Template 1, pages 7, 8) has been included for your use in two ways:

1. Use the planner as a guide in using this text. As you read through each chapter, make notes related to entry tasks specific to your school that you must consider. We suggest that you do this for each accomplishment area.

2. Use the example of the Entry Planner and your notes to construct your personal Entry Plan.

    - There are two examples that you will use: the *Entry Planner* and the *Entry Planner Calendar of Tasks*.

    - Both of these examples are included in the downloadable templates. See page xiv for details. The examples allow you to add rows and columns and to modify the format to meet your personal needs.

    - The *Entry Planner* will help you organize yourself to provide excellent and foresighted leadership for your school.

    - The *Entry Planner* provides you a way to keep track of your work and can be used as a communication tool with your leadership team and your supervisor.

Let's Get Started!

- ♦ As you read each chapter, highlight or make notes in the margin about any tasks, ideas, or responsibilities that your reading has prompted. After you complete each chapter, transfer your notes to the *Entry Planner* example. Note the target *month* that each task will require your attention. Use the hard copy in this section or use the example from the downloadable templates at http://www.eyeoneducation.com

- ♦ Next, use the *Entry Planner Calendar of Tasks* (Template 2, pages 9, 10) to organize the activities chronologically. Once you have done this, you will have a weekly agenda that includes every task or responsibility you must accomplish before the school year begins and during the first few weeks of the school year.

As you fill out your Entry Planner, you may be surprised at the quantity of management tasks that need attention. Some of these can be delegated to other appropriate personnel. Others cannot or will still require your careful review prior to implementation. It is important to recognize that if the management tasks are not addressed well, they will eventually take up the time any principal might have hoped to invest on instructional issues. Using the Entry Planner will surface thinking that will allow you to decide which of these tasks you may delegate with confidence. This level of organization frees you from "yellow stickies" and worry. You can attend to each task, giving it your full attention and energy. The best news is that you can proceed confidently in preparing for the new school year!

Template 1. Entry Planner (Example)

Accomplishment Area	Task/Responsibility	Target Month
Learning Goals	Review current and draft School Improvement Plans (SIPs)	May/June
	Meet with Academic Council regarding department-based goals and status	May
Instruction	Building walk-through on different routes and at different times of day	May/Aug
Student Climate	Meet with new Student Government Cabinet	May
	Informal visits with students in halls	May 25–30
	Attend graduation, end-of-year events; be present on students' last day	As scheduled—May/June
	Tour physical plant informally	Daily
	Review student survey data	June/July
	Review student handbook	June/July
Related Services	Set up meetings with providers	As scheduled—June
	Request service templates to be filled out by primary providers	As Scheduled—June
Resources Mobilized	Meet with Alumni Association President	June
	Meet with Volunteer Chairman	June
	Task secretary with completing External Resource Templates	June
	Identify and set up meetings with key contacts	June
School Operations	Meet with building manager for formal tour of plant	June
	Set up lunch meeting with my secretary	May
	Meet with data processor regarding Master Schedule	June
	Review permit status/enrollment projections	June
	Review budget/purchase status and timelines	May
	Follow up on all hiring needs	Ongoing
	Meet with Administrative Team	June
Staff Supported	Develop letter to staff inviting personal meetings; establish schedule and sign-up procedures	May
	Develop welcome/informational letter for all new hires	June
	Develop "Back to School" letter	July
	Review supervision and evaluation timelines; develop start-up material packets	June–Aug
	Meet with Staff Development Coordination Team to plan start-up activities	July
	Prep for start-up meetings	
School Renewal	Meet Building Accountability Chair to plan finalization of SIP	June
	Meet with School Leadership Team to plan finalization of SIP	May
	Collect end-of-year data/assessment data	June–Aug
	Review committee governance structure	July
Family–Community Partnerships	Meet with Parent-Teacher Organization Chair	June
	Develop letter for community/newsletter	July
	Plan start-up orientations	July

Template for the Entry Planner can be found at www.eyeoneducation.com and on page 8.

Template 1. Entry Planner

Accomplishment Area	Task/Responsibility	Target Month
Learning Goals		
Instruction		
Student Climate		
Related Services		
Resources Mobilized		
School Operations		
Staff Supported		
School Renewal		
Family–Community Partnerships		

Template 2. Entry Planner Calendar of Tasks (Example)

Task/Responsibility	Target Date	Outcome—Next Steps	"X"
Week of: May 24			
Meet with current supervisor	May 25	Transition plan developed	X
Meet with current principal	May 25	Info/transition plan in place	X
Meet with new supervisor	May 25	Info/expectations/support	X
Develop letter inviting staff for personal interviews/develop schedule/sign-up	May 25		X
Review current and draft School Improvement Plans	May 26, ongoing	Established basic familiarity for upcoming meetings	X
Meet with Student Government Cabinet	May 26, second period	Set dates for August retreat; introductions	X
Week of: May 29			
Attend graduation	May 30, 9 AM		X
Lunch meeting with secretary	May 31, 11:30 AM	Intro—Set up planning/tasks	X
Meet with Academic Council	May 31, 1 PM	Intro—Set up August work session	X
Meet with School Improvement Planning Team	May 31, 3 PM	Intro—Set up August meeting	X
Weeks of: June 5–16			
(Add rows as needed)			
Weeks of: June 19–30			
Month: July			
Month: August			
Month: September			

Template for the Entry Planner Calendar of Tasks can be found at www.eyeon education.com and on page 10.

Template 2. Entry Planner Calendar of Tasks

Task/Responsibility	Target Date	Outcome—Next Steps	"X"
Week of:			
Week of:			
Weeks of:			
(Add rows as needed)			
Weeks of:			
Month:			
Month:			
Month:			

2
Accomplishment: Defining Learning Goals

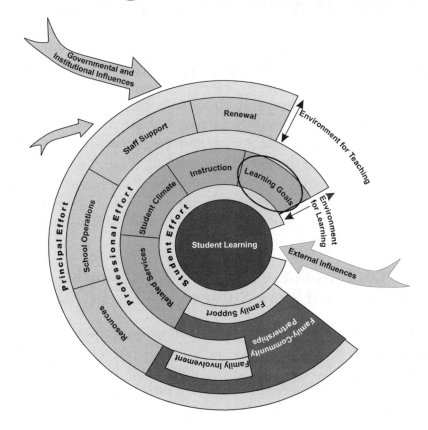

Essential Tasks

Getting "a Feel" for Your Curriculum and Programs

Building a Positive Relationship with Curricular Leaders in Your School

Building New Staff Members' Confidence and Competence with the Curriculum

Is There a Guaranteed and Viable Curriculum?

2

Defining Learning Goals

Providing the Foundation for Effective and Known Learning Goals

Getting "A Feel" for Your Curriculum and Programs

The literature on school leadership abounds with articles and books referring to the school principal as the *instructional leader* of the school. Clearly, although there are hundreds of additional tasks and responsibilities, leading quality instruction in your school is the essence of your job.

You will spend a great deal of time learning about the curriculum and instructional programs throughout your first year as principal, but are there things in this area that you should acquaint yourself with early in the school year? Let us suggest two starting points.

Review the Content Standards and Benchmarks for Each Grade Level/Core Subject

Your district may have adopted state standards and benchmarks, or it may have formatted these core guidelines to reflect a district content standards document, such as a Curriculum Map or Curriculum Alignment Guide. Whichever is applicable, you will want to ensure that you have copies of these documents available to you in your office and that you are generally familiar with the core emphasis in each of the content areas.

Schedule "Student Learning" Conversations with Staff Members

Second, you will want to schedule a time to meet with teachers in whatever configuration is most applicable (grade levels, teams, departments) during the first few weeks of school and discuss with them the essential learning goals for students attending your school. This is a time for *asking* and *listening*, rather than *telling*. By having these scheduled conversations, the message will be clear: "As principal of this school, I take student learning very seriously. I want to ensure that our written, taught, and tested curriculums are aligned. I want to ensure that as teachers you have the knowledge, skills, and resources you need to be successful. And, I want all of us to do regular monitoring of student learning and provide interventions when learning isn't taking place."

During your "student learning" conversations, you might ask teachers to respond to questions such as these. Assure them that your purpose in asking these questions is for your own learning and enlightenment, not to ask "trick questions" or to judge them. You are interested and committed to "learning about learning" in your school.

♦ How familiar are you with the content standards and benchmarks (or grade-level expectations) for the subjects and the grade levels that you teach?

♦ How do you develop your teaching plans to ensure that they are driven by the content standards and benchmarks?

♦ How do you determine what students already know and are able to do relative to the content standards and benchmarks?

♦ What have previous years' formal or informal test data told you regarding content standards or benchmarks that students find challenging and difficult to master?

♦ How do you monitor the progress of students relative to content standards and benchmarks? How is this communicated to the students and/or parents?

♦ Do all students have access to instruction of all of the content standards and benchmarks, or does this vary according to group or classroom?

♦ Do the curriculum materials that you use adequately address all of the content that students are expected to learn and are tested on, or are there gaps between the content standards and the instructional materials available to you?

The conversation that takes place anchored by these questions will give you insight into the significance and use of learning goals in your school. Likely, the conversation will also serve to inform your teachers as well, causing them to reflect on their own practices and creating awareness of their colleagues' practices and strategies. This can serve as the beginning of a continued conversation throughout the school year regarding further discussion on learning goals or moving into the areas of instruction, classroom management, student assessment, and so on.

Be sure to thank the teachers for their time, both at the time of the meeting and with a follow-up written note. Let them know your key learnings and any follow-up actions you would like to pursue to assist with needs they identified (i.e., "We don't have easily accessible copies of the standards and benchmarks";

"We haven't seen an analysis of last year's achievement scores according to standards"; "We do not have adequate materials for teaching measurement"). For your own future reference, keep a *learning goals file* with your notes in place. This will assist you when you do further work in this area.

Building a Positive Relationship with Curricular Leaders in Your School

Each school or district typically has unique structures and/or positions assigned to support the curriculum and instruction for the school. You will want to design a process and schedule to meet regularly with staff members who are responsible for this work. Oftentimes, elementary schools have instructional, literacy, or math coaches; middle schools often have team leaders; and high schools typically are staffed with department chairpersons. Depending on the job descriptions of these positions, the time allocated and compensation awarded for their work, and prior training and expectations of your predecessor, the responsibilities and effectiveness of these positions may vary greatly. You will want to meet with the individuals serving in these positions to ascertain the present status of these roles.

As with each of your encounters with existing roles and structures, it is important to "honor the old" while exploring how modifications may increase the overall effectiveness. Begin by having the persons in these leadership roles tell you about their role and responsibilities. The following are possible questions you might want to include in your discussion.

- ◆ Is there a formal job description that was given to you when you were appointed to this position? If so, how close does the job description reflect the "realities" of the position? In the areas where there are discrepancies, what are those and why do they exist?

- ◆ If there is not a formal job description, what would you define as your primary responsibilities?

- ◆ How long have you served in this position? How was the position assigned (i.e., interview process, staff rotation, voluntary, etc.)?

- ◆ What are the tasks or assignments that require the greatest amount of time for you in this position?

- ◆ How often do you meet with staff members who are a part of your team/department/grade level/curricular area? What are the structures for those meetings? What is the primary content for those meetings? How are decisions reached?

- Is there a process for identifying the essential curriculum, sharing effective instructional strategies, and developing and scoring common assessments?
- Would you describe your role as supervisory, consultancy, or collegial?
- Do you conduct classroom observations? If so, how often and for what purpose?
- What curricular accomplishments are you most proud of in the school/grade level/department?
- What do you see as the curricular needs that require the most immediate attention? If addressed, what effect do you believe this would have on student achievement?
- Have you been given specific training for this position? If so, what training did you find most effective? If not, is there training that you believe would support you in this role?
- Are there other things that you can identify that would contribute to you being even more effective in your role?
- In the past, how did you and your principal communicate regarding your work? What role did the principal play in your grade-level/team/department meetings? Were agendas and summaries of your meetings shared with the principal?
- What would you like me to do to support your success and the success of your colleagues?

In closing, be sure to thank each person for her/his time and for helping you to better understand her/his role. Emphasize how important their leadership is to the effectiveness of the school and that you appreciate their talents and commitment. Follow this up with a written communication, again acknowledging your appreciation and highlighting key aspects of the conversation.

Building New Staff Members' Confidence and Competence with the Curriculum

New teachers in your building, whether experienced or fresh out of college, typically are confronted with curriculum and instructional materials that are new to them. Prior to school starting, you will want to ensure that your new teachers have the opportunity to access curriculum documents and teacher manuals as well as meet with one or more colleagues who are responsible for teaching the same content and instructional level. Douglas Reeves, in his book *The Leader's Guide to Standards* (2002), underscores the importance of these collegial meetings by stating that "The sheer quantity of curricular requirements can be overwhelming, and every single element of those requirements feels like a mandate. Help the new teacher understand what can be dropped. Power standards are an essential concept, empowering the teacher to collaborate with colleagues to identify the most important standards." Clearly, it is important that an ongoing support system be in place for these teachers as they establish themselves in the classroom.

If there is an active and effective mentoring program in your school and district, strategies for addressing these issues may already be in place. Rather than assume, check to make sure that your new teachers have been provided with the following information and support, either by you, their mentor, or a grade-level/team/department colleague.

- Course syllabus (if applicable); essential content standards/benchmarks
- All teacher manuals and student materials
- Pretest and placement materials and procedures
- Reading and/or supply lists
- Common grade-level or course assessments and a schedule for administration
- Rubrics, checklists, scoring criteria to evaluate student work and performance
- Pacing charts (if applicable); general guidelines for the speed with which students proceed through units or chapters and the independent practice that is recommended for mastery
- Homework policy
- Sample lesson plans/resource files from more experienced teachers
- Student achievement data from previous school year(s)

Oftentimes, principals will hold "New Teacher Meetings" on a monthly basis throughout the school year to monitor their needs and provide more in-depth explanation and training in particular areas. Whatever process that you use, it's important to remember that teacher turnover most often results from teachers feeling uninformed and unsupported. When you combine support and information with a guaranteed and viable curriculum being identified as the school factor having the greatest impact on student achievement, it is essential that the entry of new teachers into the classroom be designed for success.

Is There a Guaranteed and Viable Curriculum?

In the book *What Works in Schools* (2003), researcher and author Robert Marzano identifies seven school-level factors that most significantly impact student achievement. Of the seven factors, a *guaranteed and viable curriculum* is listed as the strongest correlate with student achievement. When we think about it, this should not come as any surprise. After all, if students have not had the opportunity to learn the *content* expected of them, there is little chance that they will. Second, if there has not been enough instructional time committed to learning the most important content, learning will not be demonstrated.

Marzano suggests that school faculties use the survey excerpt given in the Snapshot Survey of School Effectiveness Factors on page 18 to reflect on the degree to which their school provides a guaranteed and viable curriculum. You might consider introducing the book *What Works in Schools* to your staff either at a faculty meeting or through particular teachers at your school who are designated as curriculum leaders (i.e., literacy coaches, instructional coaches, department chairpersons, etc). You might provide them access to that book's Chapter 2: A Guaranteed and Viable Curriculum (pages 22–34) to read and then come to your "student learning" conversation meetings with the survey completed and ready to discuss as a grade level, team, or department. Through these discussions, everyone will learn how close or how far away staff members perceive the school is in providing a guaranteed and viable curriculum and how challenging it would be to address these issues.

Again, through these conversations, ensure that you communicate through words and tone that you are not designing these discussions to find fault or assign blame but to assist the teachers in learning more about how the present curricular design is contributing to or limiting the achievement of students in your school. It is important that everyone feels that her/his input is valued and respected.

Snapshot Survey of School Effectiveness Factors

In My School	Question 1 To what extent do we engage in this behavior or address this issue?				Question 2 How much will a change in our practices on this item increase the academic achievement of our students?				Question 3 How much effort will it take to significantly change our practices regarding this issue?			
	Not at all			To a great extent	Not at all			To a great extent	Not at all			To a great extent
Guaranteed and Viable Curriculum	1	2	3	4	1	2	3	4	1	2	3	4
1. The content considered essential for all students to learn versus the content considered supplemental has been identified and communicated to teachers.												
2. The amount of essential content that has been identified can be addressed in the instructional time available to teachers.												
3. The essential content is organized and sequenced in a way that students have ample opportunity to learn it.												
4. Someone checks to ensure that teachers address essential content.												
5. The instructional time available to teachers is protected by minimizing interruptions and scheduled non-instructional activities.												

Excerpt from *What Works in Schools: Translating Research into Action*, by R. J. Marzano, 2003, Alexandria, VA: Association for Supervision and Curriculum Development. Reprinted with permission.

The Association for Supervision and Curriculum Development (ASCD) is a worldwide community of educators advocating sound policies and sharing best practices to achieve the success of each learner. To learn more, visit ASCD at www.ascd.org.

Chapter Summary

In order to ensure ambitious and comprehensive learning goals that are understood by everyone, you have gathered information from district leaders and, more importantly, from each classroom teacher in your building. This information gathering has happened in a variety of forums: individual conversations, questionnaires, and department meetings. Your goal is to ensure that you build relationships with teachers that reinforce your emphasis that learning goals are the priority in the building. Through your own information gathering, you want to assure yourself that there is a guaranteed and viable curriculum in place throughout your building. The ideas that surfaced for you while reading this chapter will make a difference for your school *only* if you act on them. Remember the Entry Planner in Chapter 1? Download the Planner right now at www.eyeon education.com or use the hardcopy on page 8. Take just five or ten minutes to list the tasks that you need to accomplish related to *Defining Learning Goals* and the target month for your attention to each task.

Now that you have made sure that you will not forget important tasks or responsibilities related to the learning goals of your school by writing them down, set aside the Planner. It is time to go on to Chapter 3, *Providing Instruction*.

3

Accomplishment: Providing Instruction

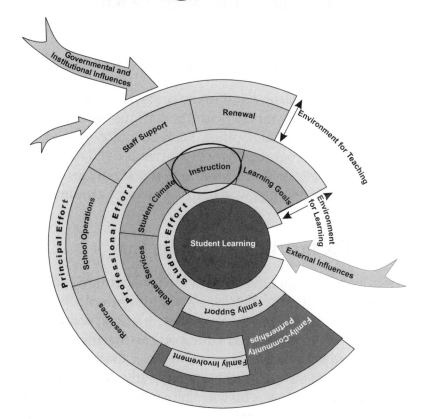

Essential Tasks

Understanding Your School's Instructional Focus

Identifying "Look For's" in the First Weeks of Instruction

Discussing Lesson Plans

Reviewing Your School's Homework Policies and Practices

3

Providing Instruction

Assessing the Status of Instruction in Your New School

Understanding Your School's Instructional Focus

Prior to the school year starting and in the first weeks of the new school year, you will want to familiarize yourself with the various aspects of your school's instructional programs and philosophies. Each school develops, over time, its own specific instructional programs to meet the needs of all of its students and its own philosophy toward lesson plans and homework policies. It is important to gain an understanding of your new school's practices around instruction and learning.

Review of Specific Instructional Programs

You may find, upon speaking with the district curriculum coordinator or your district supervisor, that either the district or your individual school has adopted a specific instructional program for mathematics, literacy, writing, or other core curriculums. It will be very important for you, as the instructional leader, to provide leadership and support to your staff in order that the programs continue and/or further develop in a successful manner. Many promising programs have floundered because the principal who was there when the adoption was initiated left the school and the incoming principal lacked the understanding, commitment, or supervisory skills to ensure the program's successful continuation. Clearly, you do not want that to occur on your watch. In preparation for a smooth and successful transition of instructional leadership, you will want to consider the following steps:

♦ Ask your supervisor or district curriculum coordinator to assist you in gaining the necessary information and/or training regarding the key programs in your building. Oftentimes, there are summer leadership trainings specific to the instructional programs. There likely is a principal leadership manual available for your review. There may be a fellow principal whose building has successfully implemented the same program who is willing to meet with you to highlight the key components of the program and the role of the principal in ensuring its success. Finally, there may be key teachers on your staff (team leaders, department chairpersons, literacy or math coaches) who, again, can instruct you on the critical attributes of the program and the necessary support required of the principal.

♦ Oftentimes, instructional programs need to be implemented with a specific schedule, daily time commitment, coordination with other support and/or grade-level teachers, etc. It will be important to ask these questions prior to altering the instructional schedule.

♦ Many programs provide principals with a checklist of "look for's" to help guide them when they conduct classroom observations. These "look for's" reflect the critical attributes of the program in order for it to yield the most successful results in student learning. Inquire if an observation guide or checklist is available.

♦ If you have new teachers entering your school, you will need to develop a strategy to avail them to the necessary training for these programs. Again, your district coordinator or supervisor can inform you of district or regional trainings that are available. If this is not possible, explore in-house training using key staff members.

♦ Plan to communicate with staff at the beginning of the school year your commitment to these programs and their successful implementation for student learning. Let them know that you will be meeting with them to inquire how the programs are going and gain feedback from them regarding how you can more effectively support them.

Instruction:
Where Is Its Place on the Staff Meeting Agenda?

From your previous years as a staff member in schools, you obviously have experienced varying models of staff meetings. Across the country, these meetings range in content, frequency, interaction, and popularity. Depending on the school and the principal, they are held at the beginning of the day or at the end of the day. They range from a "quick and dirty" 15-minute meeting to a meeting so long that you wonder if you should have brought your sleeping bag with you.

We address the general format of your staff meetings and considerations for that in Chapter 7: Organizing and Supporting School Operations, but it seems important to ask the question, "Should we have a standing agenda item that focuses on instruction?" There is not a right or wrong answer to this. As you look at the meeting formats and structures that you have in place, it may be that grade-level/team/department meetings along with scheduled staff development times adequately address and better serve to facilitate discussions on a range of instructional issues. The key thing that you will want to guard against is managerial issues overshadowing the focus on instruction.

Some schools address this balance between information sharing (which indeed is important) and a focus on instruction by alternating the focus of their staff meetings. One meeting is informational and coordination of activities/events only while the next meeting focuses on a specific instructional issue, designed to raise the level of instruction at the school. Other schools split the agenda, ensuring that time is assigned to instructional issues at every meeting.

Again, there is no right way to design your agendas. Tools to help you build your agendas are included in Chapter 9. Our intent in addressing this issue here is to place it on your radar screen. If, at the end of the school year, you were to review the agendas for staff meetings and the other meetings held with members of your staff, would instruction hold a prominent place? Where you invest your staff's time and attention indicates where your priorities lie.

Identifying "Look For's" in the First Weeks of Instruction

During those first weeks of school, you will want to spend considerable time in the MBWA (management by wandering around) process (see *A Passion for Excellence*, Peters & Austin, 1985), getting a feel for the climate in the building and the climate and instruction in the classrooms. Prior to school starting, it often is helpful to make a list of the kinds of things you are looking for during those brief, but regular, walk-throughs. This allows you to clearly assess the success of the start of the year and to provide informed feedback to your staff. Here are some possible "look for's":

- ◆ Classroom is safe and the physical arrangement of furniture supports student learning
- ◆ Positive and respectful interactions between the teacher and students, and between students and students
- ◆ Teachers teaching and students practicing classroom routines and rules
- ◆ On-task behavior of students; bell-to-bell teaching and learning
- ◆ Evidence of "joyful learning"
- ◆ Structure and organization that maximizes teaching and learning
- ◆ Learning activities focused on important learning goals
- ◆ Feedback to students is positive and specific

You can see from this list that these are indicators you can glean from spending just a few minutes in the classroom. Beginning with the "end in mind"—knowing what you want to see in those first few weeks of school—will give you a clear sense of how things are going, as well as feedback to provide to your teachers, both individually and as a staff.

Conducting Classroom Walk-Throughs

There are a number of models of classroom walk-throughs, but we would like to suggest for your consideration the Downey Walk-Through Process designed by Carolyn Downey, co-author of *The Three-Minute Classroom Walk-Through* (2004), because we think it possesses five important attributes:

- *The visit is short, focused, and informal.* Typically, it is suggested that you spend two to three minutes in a single classroom. Think about this. If you scheduled 30 minutes each day for the walk-through process, you would be able to visit 10 classrooms per day. Within the first months of the school year, you would possess a great amount of insight into your school's classrooms relative to curriculum, instruction, and climate.

- *Your observation can lead to teacher reflection.* Many times your visit will not be followed with conversation or feedback, but on those occasions that they are, they are perfect opportunities to inquire how the teacher arrived at a certain instructional or curricular decision.

- *The visit has both a curriculum and instructional focus.* You have the ability in this short stay to become informed as to *what* is being taught as well as *how* it is being taught.

- *Follow-ups occur occasionally and not after every visit.* The designer of this approach suggests that you may make 8 to 10 visits without having a follow-up conversation. You will determine the need for a follow-up conversation based on whether you have something important to share that you believe would be helpful to the teacher.

- *The observation is informal and collaborative.* While conducting these walk-throughs, it is not your purpose to evaluate but rather to observe, become informed, and get a feel for the instruction that routinely takes place in your school. Although you likely will take a few notes, this information is not used for formal evaluation and is not placed in a personnel file.

Purposes and Benefits of Conducting Walk-Throughs

Downey and colleagues (2004) cite reasons for a school principal to regularly conduct these brief walk-throughs. Those that we find particularly valuable to you, as a beginning principal, are the following:

- By spending time in the classrooms on a regular, if not daily, basis, you are sending an unequivocally clear message: As your principal, I put teaching and learning on the front burner. I am committed to ensuring quality instruction by both supporting and honoring your work in the classroom.

- The more you know about how teachers are performing and making instructional decisions in their classrooms, the more you will know about your school's operations.

- The frequent sampling of a teacher's actions gives greater validity to what you observe.

- Frequent observations often lower teacher apprehension over time, making formal observations more effective.

- You can identify common areas of decisions made by teachers in the classrooms that might be valuable to address later in meetings and staff development endeavors.

- If parents call about a concern, you have your own observational data as a basis for how the teacher operates in the classroom. You are better informed.

- It helps to identify possible individual teachers who require some immediate assistance.

Downey's Five-Step Process for the Three-Minute Walk-Through

Given this rationale, let us highlight the five-step process designed by Downey. Recognize that we are providing you an outline for this process, and we encourage you to do more in-depth reading about the process from the book *The Three-Minute Classroom Walk-Through* (2004).

- *Step 1: Student Orientation to Work.* This first step is completed in the first two seconds of your observation and hopefully before you are noticed by the students. You are observing whether or not students are attending to their work, either by listening, writing, interacting with the teacher or other students, or working alone. In other words, are students engaged in learning in some manner?

- *Step 2: Curricular Decision Points.* The majority of the visit is spent on this step. You want to know the content of what is being taught. By observing this, you will be able to determine if the objective of this lesson is aligned with the district curriculum and represents essential standards and benchmarks.

♦ *Step 3: Instructional Decision Points.* After you have determined the curricular focus, you are ready to look at the instructional strategies that are being used. What are the generic strategies you observe: questioning techniques, feedback, independent practice, etc.? You also may observe specific strategies, such as cooperative learning, note taking, problem solving, etc.

During your walk-throughs, it is recommended that you always complete the first three steps. Remember, your purpose is not to critique or judge but rather to gather data and begin to see patterns in classroom instruction. With time permitting, complete the following two steps.

♦ *Step 4: "Walk the Walls": Curricular and Instructional Decisions.* During this step, you are looking around the room to observe evidence of the teaching of previous curricular targets. This might be problem-solving steps, writing stages, student work, projects, etc.

♦ *Step 5: Safety and Health Issues.* Are there any noticeable safety or health issues that need to be addressed?

A sample Walk-Through Master Calendar is included for your possible use (Template 3, page 28). By using this or a similar form, you will readily see patterns from the routine visits you make to the classrooms in your school.

Template 3. Walk-Through Master Calendar

	Student Orientation to Work	Curricular Decision (Taught and Stated/Listed District Alignment)	Instructional Decision Points/Strategies Observed (e.g., Generic, School/District Focus, Subject Area Specific)	Walk the Walls (Evidence of Objectives; Extensions of Learning Environment)	Safety and Health Issues
Date: _____ Teacher/Subject: _____ _____	☐ High degree ☐ Medium degree ☐ Low degree				☐ No concerns ☐ Concerns to address
Date: _____ Teacher/Subject: _____ _____	☐ High degree ☐ Medium degree ☐ Low degree				☐ No concerns ☐ Concerns to address
Date: _____ Teacher/Subject: _____ _____	☐ High degree ☐ Medium degree ☐ Low degree				☐ No concerns ☐ Concerns to address
Date: _____ Teacher/Subject: _____ _____	☐ High degree ☐ Medium degree ☐ Low degree				☐ No concerns ☐ Concerns to address

Developed based upon *The Three-Minute Classroom Walk-Through*, by C. T. Downey, B. E. Steffy, F. W. English, L. E. Frase, and W. K. Paston, Jr., 2004, Thousand Oaks, CA: Corwin Press.

Template for the Walk-Through Master Calendar can be found at www.eyeoneducation.com.

Informing Your Staff about Your Walk-Through Practice

If you decide that walk-throughs are a valuable process to embed into your regular schedule, you will want to inform your staff of this practice. You may or may not know the observation routines of your predecessor, but your teachers will clearly feel more comfortable if they know how your practices will differ from what they have known before and your purposes for stopping by. Here are a few talking points that you may consider in providing them with this information.

♦ I want you to know that it will be my intent to stop by each of the classrooms on a regular basis for a short period of time. I hope that you will see me at least once a week in your classrooms.

♦ Let me tell you, first of all, what the purposes of these visits are *not*: they are *not* part of the evaluation process. If you are on the formal evaluation cycle, we will be meeting in the next couple of weeks to go over that process. They are *not* to judge or critique your teaching, and they are *not* in any way intended to make you feel uncomfortable.

♦ Indeed, the purposes of my visits to your classrooms are just the opposite. First of all, I believe that the most important thing that occurs at our school is your teaching and our students' learning, and through these visits, it is my intent to attend to and honor what is most important. I have been a teacher in schools where there were months, even years, when the principal did not enter my classroom. I felt that the message the principal sent was that what the teacher and her/his students do is not important to the principal. I am committed to not sending that same message to you.

♦ Second, I am new here, and I have a great deal to learn and you have a great deal to teach me. One of the best ways for me to learn about learning in our school is for me to be in classrooms regularly, hopefully almost every day. By knowing more about your teaching and your students, we will be able to engage, both individually and as groups, in discussions that will bring about even greater achievement of our students.

♦ When I stop in, I will be in your classrooms only a few minutes, unless you indicate to me that you would like me to stay longer because of something that you'd like me to observe. While I'm there for those few minutes, I'll be looking at three main things: the engagement of the students, the content of your teaching, and the methods that you use. Obviously, this is the meat of your lessons: What do I teach today, how do I teach it, and are my students engaged in their own learning?

By visiting your classrooms, I know you will teach me an incredible amount about our curriculum, our instruction, and our students' approach to learning.

♦ Probably following most visits, I'll just wave and be on my way. I won't follow up with you unless it seems important or unless you would like to talk with me about that particular visit. Certainly, after a number of visits, I would enjoy sitting with you briefly just to ask you to reflect on your teaching and tell me more about your work.

♦ I want to thank you, in advance, for making me feel welcome in your classroom. Again, this is not evaluative but rather collegial. Although I hope I contribute to your learning in the future, what I know is that you all will be contributing to my learning each time I enter your classroom.

Discussing Lesson Plans

You will want to determine from your key instructional leaders or through a conversation with your predecessor what the expectations were regarding lesson plans. Were written lesson plans required to be submitted to the principal? Was there an agreed upon format to follow? Were lesson plans shared in grade-level or department meetings? It would be our advice initially to follow whatever norms have been established in this area and to monitor this during the first semester. Later on in the first semester, you will be in a position to have a conversation with staff members regarding whether the present planning policy is working and if changes need to be made. Although many principals view lesson plans as a form of necessary accountability, it is important to recognize that the primary purpose of lesson plans is to serve as a tool for teachers to support their essential curriculum and effective instruction. Therefore, the format of the lesson plan should involve significant input from the teaching staff.

Clearly, it is important that if written lesson plans are not required to be submitted to the principal, then the staff understands that it is essential to have comprehensive plans developed and easily available to a substitute teacher when that is required.

Reviewing Your School's Homework Policies and Practices

Homework is an integral part of the educational process. In addition to serving the important purpose of providing practice and application of essential academic skills, it helps to develop responsibility and good study habits. It is unlikely that you will find many teachers or parents who disagree with the value of homework, but there is a wide spectrum of views as to how much; how often; what type; the role of the parent, student, and teacher; and the consequences for not completing homework. It becomes even more problematic if there is not a clear policy and procedure for use of homework.

Before the school year begins, you will want to become informed of your school's policies and practices around homework. If there is a stated policy, is it communicated to all faculty, students, and parents? Does it appear in your student handbook? If there is not a policy, what are the practices that presently exist? You can become informed of these practices through discussions with your teachers at the appropriate levels of meetings (i.e., grade level/teams/departments). The key information that you want to glean from these initial discussions is:

♦ What are the homework policies and practices that presently exist?

♦ How are they communicated?

♦ How are they working for the students, the teachers, and the parents?

It is unlikely that, at this time in your first year, you will want to go beyond information gathering regarding the status of homework in your school. Of course, if you find that this is a hot issue for staff or parents, then you will want to take further action. Recognize that many people have strong feelings about homework, so at the time that you address it, you will want to ensure that you design it in such a way that you guarantee the proper sharing of information, opportunities for input and discussion, and a process for reaching consensus.

For your information, we have enclosed a sample Homework Policy (page 32). This sample policy appears in the book *A Handbook for Classroom Instruction that Works* (2001, p. 121), authored by Marzano, Norford, Paynter, Pickering, and Gaddy. This handbook, along with its parent book, *Classroom Instruction that Works* (2001), authored by Marzano, Pickering, and Pollock, provides a concise summary on the key research findings regarding homework as well as a number of practical exercises and models. These materials would serve you well at a time that you determine the need to create a study team to examine homework practices in your school.

Homework Policy

This letter explains the homework policy for my classroom. Please read the policy with your child so that you understand the expectations of students and parents with regard to homework. Following these guidelines can help decrease tension associated with homework and increase your child's learning.

For your child to be successful with homework, he needs:

A place to do homework. If possible, your child should do his homework in the same place (an uncluttered, quiet space to study).

A schedule for completing homework. Set a homework schedule that fits in with each week's particular activities.

Encouragement, motivation, and prompting. It is not a good idea to sit with your child and do homework with him. Your child needs to practice independently and to apply what he has learned in class. If your child consistently cannot complete homework assignments alone, please contact me.

Understanding of the knowledge. When your child is practicing a skill, ask which steps he finds difficult and easy and how he plans to improve speed and accuracy with the skill. If your child is working on a project, ask what knowledge he is using to complete the work. If your child consistently cannot answer these questions, please contact me.

Reasonable time expectations. If your child seems to be spending too much time each night on homework, please contact me.

A bedtime. When it is time to go to bed, please stop your child, even if he has not finished the homework.

Grading: I will grade each homework assignment for content and timeliness. If your child turns in an assignment late, the score for "timeliness" will reflect the lateness.

Please return this policy with the appropriate signatures, acknowledging that you have read and discussed the policy with your child. If you have any questions about homework expectations, please contact me.

_____ ___   _____

Parent's (or Guardian's) Signature   Student's Signature

Excerpt from *A Handbook for Classroom Instruction that Works* (p. 121), by R. J. Marzano, J. S. Norford, D. E. Paynter, D. J. Pickering, and B. B. Gaddy, 2001, Alexandria, VA: Association for Supervision and Curriculum Development. Reprinted with permission of McREL.

Chapter Summary

In order to ensure that the instruction provided in your school is meeting the learning needs of all students in your building, you have carefully examined the programs and instructional practices in your school. Part of your review has focused on specific instructional programs to examine their implementation in your building and their effectiveness in meeting the academic needs of your students. You also have examined the place that instruction has on your staff meeting agenda; does instruction hold a prominent place in discussion when all staff is gathered? You have observed firsthand the instructional practices of teachers in your building by conducting walk-throughs in the first weeks of school. The short and informal walk-throughs give you an opportunity to view classroom routines, interactions between teacher and students and between students and students, and the quality of learning activities. Finally, you have reviewed your teachers' practices in developing lesson plans and homework policies: Do these practices reflect best practices in instruction, and will they foster student achievement?

It is again time to bring out your Entry Planner. Make the notes you need for *Providing Instruction* along with the target months for your attention to each task you list.

4

Accomplishment: Sustaining Student Climate

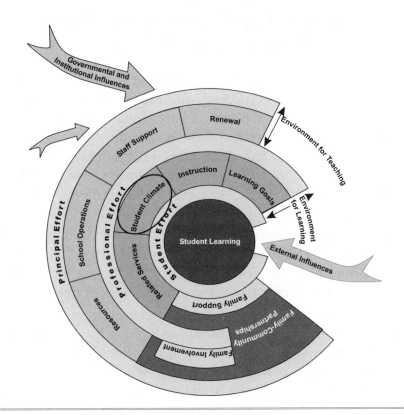

Essential Tasks

Understanding How Your Students Perceive Their School

Setting the Stage and Establishing the Tone for the School Year

Building Productive Relationships with Students

Implementing Clever Ideas to Enhance Student Climate

4

Sustaining Student Climate

Gauging and Contributing to Positive Student Climate

Understanding How Your Students Perceive Their School

All schools try to build a supportive, productive, and welcoming learning environment for students. Some succeed, and others do not. The adults associated with a school sometimes see things differently than the students see them. Student climate is *what students perceive from the sum of the implicit messages we give them about what we consider to be important.* Student climate is *each student's understanding* of the messages we give them. So, how do we know if the messages we are trying to give are understood the way they are intended?

School employees, after being in a school over time, can take things for granted. Just like living in a home for a long time, we begin to overlook the nicks and scratches on the walls because we are comfortable there. But are others? In a school, it is important that we not *assume* anything. As a newcomer to your school, you may be able to look objectively at indicators of the student climate.

You will want to acquaint yourself with the learning environment of your school. The information you can gather about your school's learning environment depends on when you receive your appointment. If your appointment occurs in the summer, there are no students in the school. You are unable to talk to them, ask them questions, and watch how they behave, learn, and interact with each other and the adults in the school. Some indicators, however, are available to you. We recommend that you invest time:

1. Walking through the entirety of the physical plant

2. Reviewing the student handbook

3. Reviewing any student survey data available

The Facility:
Is It an Environment for Teaching and Learning?

Before you tour the facility, sit down and list the kinds of things you would expect to see in a school where:

+ Students thrive academically and developmentally,

+ Teachers and staff are enthusiastic about student learning and have what they need to create extraordinary learning experiences for children,

+ Parents and community members are actively involved in the education of children.

It is time to take a walk through the entire facility. If you were fortunate enough to be appointed before the year ended, that is the best time to walk through. If you were appointed during the summer, bulletin boards and other climate enhancers may be taken down. Nonetheless, tour the facility.

☑ Check off the things on your list that you see.

O Circle those things on your list that are missing but could be addressed over the summer.

☐ Unmarked items on your list may be things that can be focused on over time through budgeting and working with others.

Now, put yourself in your students' shoes. When you walked through the facility, what observations did you make? What implicit messages did those observations give you?

Example:

Observation: The facility just shines.

Implicit message: This is a clean and healthy place to be. People here take pride in the surroundings. I need to respect that.

As you plan over the summer, be certain to keep your circled items handy. Make plans to follow through on them.

The Student Handbook:
What Messages Does It Give?

The student handbook is one of the first documents that students and parents see that represents your school. It is important that the messages in this handbook are an accurate reflection of the school and that it provides important information for the users. As the new principal, it is essential that you understand the information contained in the manual.

We suggest that you carefully review the student handbook. The attributes listed below describe many characteristics of quality handbook publications.

♦ The handbook is attractive, inviting, and organized in a way that is easy to follow.

♦ The information included is relevant, accurate, and complete.

♦ The tone is welcoming and warm.

♦ When reading this handbook, it is clear that learning is important.

♦ The language is understandable, jargon-free, and clear.

♦ The document is legible, accurate, concise, and error-free.

The Handbook for the upcoming school year is probably already in print. As you review the current handbook, keep notes for any changes in your folder(s) for **next year's planning**. If any of those proposed changes requires work with staff, students, or parents in order to implement in the future, make note and follow through.

Student Survey Data: What Can We Learn?

Students receive messages about school and learning from a variety of sources. It is important for the principal to understand how students perceive the messages that the school is giving. One way to find out is to invest time asking students questions like:

♦ What is the most important thing at our school?

♦ Who do you go to at school if you need help?

♦ What about our school helps you to learn?

♦ What about our school distracts you from learning?

♦ Do other students and adults want you to be successful? How do you know?

If the students currently are on vacation for summer, another strategy you can use to "listen" to them is to carefully review the most recent student survey. Although you may choose to modify this survey in the future, your task now is to use what is currently available to find out how students see and understand the messages that the school gives them. If there is no student survey in place at your new school, this is something that we recommend you put in place for the future.

If student survey data are available, the following questions may guide your review:

1. What process was used to survey students? What grade levels were surveyed? What percentage of the student body completed the survey?

- Answers to these questions will help put the results in perspective.

2. What are the five greatest strengths of the school as perceived by the students?

3. What are the five greatest concerns of the school as perceived by the students?

4. How can you use this information with students, parents, and staff so that they:

   - know you have done your homework and are concerned about how the students view their school?

   - understand things that need to be prioritized for attention and why?

   - can be actively involved in making needed changes?

   - celebrate the positives?

5. How can you use this information to support your leadership for the school?

Setting the Stage and Establishing the Tone for the School Year

You have hopefully had the opportunity over the summer to review the student handbook, the facility, available survey data, and other artifacts that have helped you to better understand the student climate in your school. You are also aware of the activities that are typical at your school for starting the school year. There may be traditional ceremonies or events. It will be important for you to ask staff members and your administrative team about these events.

- What involvement in these events did the previous principal have?

- What other staff is involved in these activities?

- How are the events typically organized?

- What role does *tradition* play in these events?

You will notice that the word "tradition" is intentionally emphasized. One common mistake new principals make is not being aware of traditions that are very important to students, staff, and the school community. Your stakeholders want to be reassured that you value their school community and honor their traditions. Your ability to do that will send a clear message that you are proud to be the leader of this special school community.

In her book *The 20 Biggest Mistakes Principals Make and How to Avoid Them* (2004), Marilyn Grady, lists "Ignoring the Preparation" as one of those mistakes. It is critically important that you prepare well for your first interactions with students. The question that you now need to address is: "How are you going to infuse your new understandings of the school, the value messages that you want students to have, and the information that students need as the year begins?"

To help you prepare, we recommend that you take the following action steps:

- List the start-up events and activities for students on a calendar.
- Collect the agendas or programs from last year's events and activities
- Study the agendas and programs to ascertain the degree to which students will have received the messages that provide needed information and establish a positive tone for the year.
- Work with appropriate staff to rework agendas and programs to infuse the tone, information, and messages you have identified.
- Determine your level of involvement in start-up activities.
- Develop *quality* materials necessary to provide direction for staff, documents for students, and any presentation materials that you will use.
- Take your time in thoughtfully preparing yourself, involved staff, and the materials for start-up events. The quality of activities and materials will leave lasting impressions on students and staff. You want those impressions to inspire confidence in your competency and to open doors to relationship building.

The next step in your preparation is to consider what students need to hear as they start their year. Some general topics come to mind immediately. Students are going to want to hear:

- Pride and praise for their school
- Excitement from you about working with them
- Changes in rules that may have been made and why
- The fact that fairness is important to you
- Students' safety and student learning are high priorities

Other specific information could include:

- An overview of important information in the student handbook
- Where to go to get help
- A short list of basic expectations of students and staff
- Strategies that students can use to ask questions or voice concerns
- Ways that students can access the principal
- Ways students can get involved in the school
- Upcoming celebrations
- Sharing results from last year's student survey or test results

Building Productive Relationships with Students

The messages you initially give students will be lasting and can greatly support your work on their behalf or they can become an obstacle. Your preparation will make a key difference.

Below is a list of strategies that principals use to build relationships with students. There is no "magic bullet" or one-size-fits-all method. Most principals have a handful of strategies from this menu that work for them in their efforts to build positive relationships with their students. You need to determine what works well for you. What fits your style, allows you to be genuine with your students, and promotes their effort in school? You will try many things, and, after time, you will find what works best for you and your students.

- ♦ **Student Orientations Before the School Year Begins**

  Some schools have orientations only for new students and entry grades. For example, elementary schools may have special orientations for kindergartners, whereas middle schools help their sixth-graders and high schools focus on freshmen. Other schools have orientations for entering grade levels and conduct other events aimed at taking care of paperwork, meeting teachers, or social events for the remainder of their students. It is not unusual to see these events occurring prior to the first day of school, particularly at the secondary level. The tolerance and support of the school community are critical for any event occurring prior to students' first day of school. The primary benefits include reducing new student anxiety and preventing interruption of instructional time that otherwise would be taken to do these activities. The major obstacles are assuring timely communication with families during the summer and assuring good attendance.

- ♦ **Beginning-of-the-Year Assemblies**

  Full school or large group assemblies can be an effective way to raise school spirit and give general messages of support to students. They are less effective for giving specific information that you expect students to remember. Large numbers make it difficult to engage students. However, many schools rely on an assembly format to start the year in the same way for all students.

- ♦ **Grade-Level Meetings**

  Grade-level meetings led by the principal can be extremely effective in allowing the principal to direct appropriate remarks and information to each grade level. If the number of students is too large, principals can have several grade-level meetings for each grade. The smaller the group, the greater the likelihood of engaging students in a conversational or activity-oriented format. Students are able to interact directly with the principal. They feel valued to have the principal's direct attention.

♦ **Visits to Every Classroom to Talk to Students**

This probably is the most effective way to interact personally with the greatest number of students. Students have the greatest likelihood of asking questions that are important to them and understanding information that you are giving them. The small group allows the principal to provide the information in a variety of ways that can include activities, small groups rotating through stations, and discussion groups, among other strategies. The downside of this approach is the amount of time required of the principal to go to every single classroom.

♦ **After-School Social Events**

During the first week of school, principals can organize picnics, ice cream socials, and other events to meet students. This kind of setting affords a social setting to meet, greet, and build relationships with students. It is not a good setting for presenting detailed information or re-iterating school rules. These events, at elementary and middle school levels, can be used to build relationships among students and with the principal and teachers. At the high school level, these events are primarily used for building camaraderie among students and secondarily provide visibility and a venue for the principal to interact with students and staff.

♦ **Meeting With Student Clubs and Organizations**

These kinds of meetings provide a great opportunity for the principal to listen to student ideas and to interact in a personal way with students having a common interest. It is also a venue that can be used to help students connect their interests with the school's initiatives. It is not a good setting for restating information that you have provided to students in other forums. This strategy will not allow principals to interact with the greatest number of students in the school, but it does allow conversation with students who are active in the school.

♦ **Lunch in the Cafeteria**

Many principals set up days of the week when they will go to eat with students in the cafeteria. This allows the principal to select students she/he will sit with. It is a good time to interact with students who are not involved in the school. The vigilant principal will spread attention to as many groups of students as possible. Otherwise, students quickly jump to the conclusion that time is spent only with certain groups of students.

Simply being in the cafeteria for part of every lunch period provides visibility for the principal and a time for casual conversation with students during the walk-through. Random walk-through visits to the cafeteria and classrooms also tend to promote positive behavior from students.

♦ **Student Forums**

Principals need to identify strategies that will allow them to "keep the pulse" of student attitudes, concerns and perceptions of the school. Particularly at the secondary level, it is common to find that principals have established representative groups of students with whom they meet regularly. There are numbers of ways to create these forum groups. Some principals ask classes during a specific time period of the day to nominate one student per class for the forum. The principal establishes a topic for the day. Classes take a few moments to generate their thoughts and concerns related to the topic. The representatives present at the forum while the principal listens and responds. Representatives return to class and report out.

These kinds of forums allow students a venue to voice concerns and can engage the entire school in regular conversations about important school issues.

♦ **Video Announcement Segments**

Some schools produce video announcements on a daily or weekly basis. Principals can be involved in segments of the news program to make special announcements or simply to be in sketches that may be included. It is a good thing for students to see the principal's human side, too.

♦ **Daily Announcements**

Principals in many schools give the daily announcements to the student body. This allows students to hear from the principal daily. In high schools, principals may be part of the announcement program, but generally it is the privilege of the student organization or other selected groups to give announcements.

♦ **Greeting Students as They Arrive**

Regardless of the age of the student, being greeted by the principal at the bus or as parents drop you off gives an important message. This is a time for casual interaction with students, parents, the bus drivers, and other staff.

♦ **Classroom Visits**

The principal's presence in classrooms is critical. Whether scheduled or unscheduled, your visibility in classrooms gives an important message to students and staff; learning is important!

There are many ways to interact regularly with students. It is important for you to design your own repertoire of strategies and to use them consistently.

Implementing Clever Ideas to Enhance Student Climate

Start-Up Assemblies

Assemblies at the beginning of the year can be fairly predictable. The ideas below can jazz them up a little while further reinforcing the important messages.

- **Dress Code Fashion Shows**

  Arrange with student volunteers (student council groups and others) to illustrate the do's and don'ts of the dress code. A little fashion show in an assembly can be fun and a good learning experience.

- **Rules Skits**

  The older that students get, the more they seem to question the rules. The older grades at each level can develop skits about the rules that illustrate the do's and don'ts. The narrator can also explain the why's between skits.

- **School Pride**

  A variety of strategies can be used to develop a sense of pride in the school.

At the **elementary** level, doing cheers with the school mascot or learning songs that use the school name and incorporate positive messages about behavioral or academic expectations are popular and useful. Many schools use the school name or mascot name as an acronym to describe important messages. For example: The LIONS.

L   Learning opens doors

I   I care about myself and others

O   Owning my behavior shows how responsible I am

N   New ideas help me listen and learn to ask good questions

S   Striving to do my best helps me grow

At the **secondary** level, focusing on pride in the school and pride in the grade level is typical. Seating students in sections by grade level and having cheerleaders lead cheers by grade level are fun and can be competitive. Chain ropes with each link being a day of school can be created for each grade at the high school level. At each assembly, the class representative tears off the number of days appropriate so that the chains grow shorter and shorter as the year goes on. Freshmen have chains that equal four years of school, sophomores have three years, and so on. You can also do this in reverse, so that the chains get longer by grade level and illustrate days of learning. When the chain reaches a certain length, it is time to graduate. These assemblies are also good venues to recognize varieties of student groups and their achievements.

Tradition-Building Activities

♦ **Traveling Reading Tour**

Orienteering courses can be set up around the school. Descriptions of important places in the building can be posted by checkpoints. Students follow the course and learn about their school. They read their way. Follow-up classroom activities reinforce the learnings.

♦ **Alumni Lessons and Tours**

Many schools are fortunate enough to have alumni associations or parent organizations that are willing to give classes tours of the facility and lessons about its history and traditions. Elementary schools can do this by class. Secondary schools can do this through a content area. These activities are geared particularly well for entering grade levels. The fact that a community member is giving positive messages about the school is impactful.

♦ **Scavenger Hunts**

Hunts lend themselves to familiarization with the facility, resources, and staff.

♦ **Writing Activities**

Writing activities can be constructed around topics of importance at your school. Students can be grouped so that each group is investigating a particular topic. The students interview staff, students, or parents about the topic and prepare a written summary. The summaries are compiled in the group and edited into a final summary. Each group presents their findings to the class.

♦ **Interviews and Writing/Presenting**

Learning about the staff members who provide specific support for students is important. Using a format similar to the one described above, students can be assigned a staff member to interview and learn about.

♦ **Video Displays**

Video loops about the school or school events can be played in display cases along with appropriate displays of artifacts. These displays are interesting and informative for students, staff, and community members who come into your building. Some schools have classes that allow students to design video segments.

♦ **Spotlights on Students**

These show that students are valued and celebrated. For example, in schools with English as a Second Language programs, students from various parts of the world can be spotlighted. They bring items for the display case and write essays that will be posted next to their items and picture. Changing these displays frequently will allow schools to celebrate wide varieties of students and cultures over a year's time.

♦ **Birthday Button Decorations**

Student organization groups or staff create birthday buttons. These are construction paper shapes of the school mascot or geometric shapes. Each student's name is printed with his/her birthday written beneath the name. The buttons are posted all over the school on the hallway or classroom walls. These can be randomly scattered around the school or organized by months.

♦ **Letters to New Students**

Unexpected letters from alumni, students, parents, the principal, or other staff members can be a very special welcome to a new school.

♦ **Picture Walls**

Picture walls are easy to make. Find a conspicuous wall in the main office or other supervised area of the building. Install indoor/outdoor carpet directly to the wall. Mount hook-and-loop strips in an appealing arrangement on the carpet. Have pictures of student taken frequently in learning and co-curricular activities. As they are developed, select a variety of pictures. Using the other side of the hook-and-loop tape, mount the pictures to the picture wall. A 5 × 7 size works well. Change the pictures every two weeks. Write personal messages on the back of the pictures you are taking down and give them to the pictured students.

Focusing on Achievement

♦ **Student Exemplars**

Save student work at the end of each year. Have these items ready to display prior to the beginning of school. When students enter the building on the first day, they see student work up already.

♦ **Recognition Walls and Displays**

Permanent displays can be created to celebrate attributes that are important in your school or special achievements. Changing the displays frequently allows you to recognize great numbers of students throughout the year.

♦ **Surprise Visits for Recognition**

Principals can ask teachers to recommend students for recognition. The principal shows up in a classroom and recognizes the student in front of her/his peers. Genuine recognition from the principal sends the message that the principal is aware of students' achievements and finds them valuable enough to take time to recognize them.

♦ **Work for Rewards Programs**

There are varieties of these kinds of programs. Most of them are founded on providing incentives for academic improvement. Improvement may be defined by grade point average improvements, test score improvements, or attendance improvements. For example, in one school, business partners sponsor students who have improved their performance in a way defined by the school and the partner. In this case it was grade point improvement of 0.5 to qualify. The business started a savings account for each student. For every grading period that the student continues to show improvement, the partner makes another deposit. Upon graduation, the money is given to the student. If the student drops out, she/he forfeits the account, and the money is used for other students.

Support Activities

♦ **Older Student Buddy Programs**

Programs that invest time in training older students to "buddy" with incoming students can make a difference. Structuring the program is important. Otherwise, regardless of good intentions, students can forget to follow through. These programs take many different shapes. Some schools have structured peer counseling programs. Others invest in transition programs for incoming students that primarily focus on orientation type activities. Resources to support these programs usually determine the school's choice of program.

♦ **Help Matrix**

Development of a support guide that students can carry in notebooks and parents can post on the refrigerator is very useful. These guides typically categorize the services (i.e., Homework Help, Counseling, etc.), describe them, and list contact names and phone numbers.

♦ **Planners Embedded in Curriculum**

Student planners can be useful tools if they are used everyday in every class. It is important to generate staff support for this activity to maximize the payoff for your investment.

♦ **Counseling Series**

Counseling programs can design a series of activities for students in classes. Topics are developed, and tools to help students are created. For example, one topic might be organizing materials. Counselors make class visits and teach students how to organize their materials. Counselors circulate through all classes until each student has been helped. The cycle begins again with the next topic.

♦ **Success Classes/Sessions**

There are a wide variety of programs that can be purchased and implemented in schools to help students. There are also great numbers of programs that have been developed in schools using their own initiative and materials. Success classes can take the form of classes that are required of all students (i.e., ninth-grade study skills), classes that are scheduled to meet the needs of students requiring specific academic intervention (reading or math intervention programs), or sessions that are voluntary for students.

Chapter Summary

In order to ensure that the climate in your school is conducive to student learning, you have "taken the pulse" of the school climate. You have examined the building from the perspective of students: What does the physical facility communicate to students? Is the building clean, is student work exhibited, does the building reflect a pride in the people who work there and the work that is accomplished? You have also looked at various messages sent implicitly and explicitly to students in the student handbook, and you have reviewed information from student surveys to gain an insight into their perception of the school. All of this information gathering allows you to set the tone for the upcoming school year. The various activities you plan for the year—student orientation, assemblies, student forums, classroom visits, tradition-building activities, etc.—all are opportunities to create an atmosphere of safety, trust, and healthy relationships. Your goal is to build productive relationships with students that lead to increased academic performance. Remember to use your Entry Planner!

5
Accomplishment: Providing Related Services

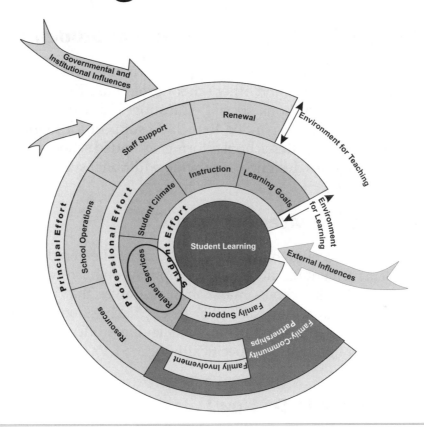

Essential Tasks

Identifying Related Services for Students

Helping Staff, Students, and Parents Know What Is Available

Helping Staff Access Support Services

Helping Parents and Students Access Support Services

Assuring That Students Get the Help They Need in Time—On time

5

Providing Related Services

Examining Your School's Related Services

Identifying Related Services For Students

Related services in a school are the supports provided to students that help them benefit from instruction and other school programs. These have traditionally been identified primarily as special education and Title I services. More recently these services have expanded to include support for English language learners, before-school and after-school tutoring, extended school year programs, and other school programs designed to provide additional support to contribute to student success.

Why Are Related Services Important?

In this era of high accountability, school success has been redefined to reflect high levels of achievement for all students. Emphasis on narrowing the achievement gap has resulted in schools marshaling resources that allow previously underserved students to achieve at higher levels. Each school now is asked to clearly identify those populations of underachieving students and their needs and to design programs that are specifically tailored to contribute to student academic success.

What Do You Need to Do Now?

Initially, it is most important that you become aware of all related services provided to the students in your school. You will not have time to grasp every detail of each support right now. As the year progresses, you will be able to invest time in clearly understanding each service and its impact on the achievement of the students it serves.

It is also important that you begin to collect data associated with each related service for your reference and later study of service impacts.

In order for you accomplish these tasks, we strongly recommend that you take the following steps:

- ♦ Ask your secretary, an Assistant Principal (if you are fortunate enough to have one), staff member in charge of assessment, or another appropriate staff member to:

  - Develop a list of all related services provided in your school. A list of common related services is included (page 52) for your reference and the reference of those you charge with this responsibility.

- ♦ Review district policies to see if there are standards of quality adopted or endorsed for each service.

- ♦ Make a file folder for each related service. An example, *Organizing Information About Related Services,* is provided for you (Template 4, page 53). In each folder, the staff member will collect:

  - Related service description

  - List of service providers, staff member responsible, and contact information

  - Description of students receiving service and student list, if necessary

  - Any data associated with the service/students served

  These files will be a valuable and ready resource for you now and over time. As new data become available, they can be added to the file. As you begin to have student learning discussions with program staff, you will have a ready reference.

Once the information is available, use the questions below to assist your understanding of each related service, of the scope of service provided, of the students involved, and to analyze available data to determine service impacts.

Your analysis will also enable you to develop questions that you can study over the course of the school year and to identify strengths and needs in service provisions to students in your school.

Guiding Questions to Analyze Related Services

It is important that you look at your school's data trends and most current student achievement data as explained in Chapter 9: Supporting School Renewal. As part of that task, you will identify achievement gaps and needed focus areas.

1. Which Adequate Yearly Progress (AYP) groups are receiving related services?

   - Are the services appropriate to the performance needs illustrated by the available data?

   - If not, what are the gaps?

2. Does the draft of this year's School Improvement Plan (SIP) include goals that serve students receiving related services?

- If so, are the services aligned to support achievement of the goal? Do they need to be?

- Are the related service providers included in the activities listed with the goal? Is their involvement appropriate?

- If the services are not aligned or the providers are not included, do you need to involve representatives from the related service providers in reviewing and/or modifying the goal/activities/responsibilities?

3. What is in place to monitor the impact of related services on student performance and achievement?

- Does the data available for monitoring give you and the service providers the information needed to assure continuous service improvement?

- If not, what would?

4. What questions do you need to seek the answers to over the course of this upcoming school year?

Common Related Services for Students

- Academic Intervention Programs
- Alternative Programs
- Attendance Intervention Program
- Behavior Modification Program
- Career Development Program
- Counseling
- Deaf Education Program
- English as a Second Language
- Extended Day Care
- Extended School Year Programs
- Free and Reduced Breakfast and Lunch Program
- Group Counseling/Support (Substances, Pregnancy, etc.)
- Math Intervention Program
- Medical Services on site
- Nursery
- Physical Therapy
- Reading Intervention Program
- Social Work
- Special Education Services
- Speech Services
- Title I
- Tutorials
- Work-Study Programs

Template 4. Organizing Information about Related Services (Example)

Related Service Title:	Summer Institute	
Service/Program Description:		

The Summer Institute will occur the three weeks preceding the beginning of the school year. It is taught by reading specialists and involves specific reading intervention programs to meet specific student needs. Class sizes are no larger than 15. Pre and post assessments will be given to track program impact on each student's growth in reading.

- Corrective Reading mandatory for low-level decoders (more than 3 years below grade level).
- Read 180 assigned for high-level decoders but low-level comprehension and fluency (2–3 years below grade level).

A second component of the program is transition to the high school. Upperclassmen involved and trained as Link Crew Leaders will conduct relationship and informational activities with these students.

The program is subsidized by the central office.

Service Providers:	Contact Information	
	Office Phone	**Office E-mail**
Steve Stevens Primary-Literacy Resource Teacher	222-3333	sstevens@d1000.org
Mary Barry, Reading Specialist	222-4444	mbarry@d1000.org
Larry Lowe, Reading Specialist	222-5555	llowe@d1000.org

Students Served Description (attach list if necessary):

The program is designed for incoming Individual Literary Plan (ILP) students needing intense focused work on reading skills. This year, the program involves incoming freshmen only and is based on last spring's ILPs. Staff met with the students and parents to develop buy-in. The 45 students involved volunteered and paid $25 for the three-week experience.

Data Included in File:

- Pre and Post Results from Summer Institute
- Student State Assessment Results in Reading (previous two years)
-
-
-

Template for Organizing Information about Related Services can be found at www.eyeoneducation.com and on page 54.

Template 4. Organizing Information about Related Services

Related Service Title:		
Service/Program Description:		

Service Providers:	Contact Information	
	Office Phone	**Office E-mail**

Students Served Description (attach list if necessary):

Data Included in File:

- ■
- ■
- ■
- ■
- ■

Helping Staff, Students, and Parents Know What Is Available

One common mistake new principals make is to *assume* that staff members in the building have an understanding of available support services. During start-up of the school year, it is imperative that all staff know what support is available *and* how and when to access it. The same holds true for parents and students. A support service in one family's experience may be very different from the same service in your school. For example, a tutoring program in the feeder elementary school that your incoming sixth-graders participated in last year will likely operate differently than does yours. It is important to get information to parents and students so that they will know what to expect from your programs. If you do not tend to this, parents and students will operate from their personal experience base and may make *assumptions* about your programs. This often precipitates misunderstandings that you will ultimately have to invest time rectifying later.

The annual start-up of schools requires some things being in place and made known to staff, parents, and students:

- ♦ Annual updates at the beginning of each year will serve both new and current staff in better meeting the needs of students in the school.

- ♦ Information and user-friendly reference material about support services must be provided to all parents and students.

- ♦ Procedures for quickly identifying students needing support services should be refined and updated annually.

Helping Staff Access Support Services

Staff members work with students everyday. They can identify quickly those students who are having difficulty learning in class and in many cases can make modifications in instruction or materials to help these students. Sometimes, the time they are investing is a duplication of services that are available elsewhere in the school. Other times, regardless of the strategies they attempt, the student continues to struggle. The frustration for the student, who cannot seem to grasp the learning, and the frustration for the teacher, who is trying every strategy she/he knows and still cannot help the student, can initiate a self-defeating cycle for both of them. If teachers understand services that are available to help them or to help students, they are likely to access them.

Annual updates at the beginning of each year will serve both new and current staff in better meeting the needs of students in the school. These updates should include:

- Description of each service
- Description of student needs that are served through each service
- Referral procedures and timelines
- Contact information for service provider(s)

It is helpful for all staff to have this information organized by categories and in written form for continual reference. Do not expect, however, that simply handing out the information will translate to teachers taking time during start-up to read and understand it. Instead, we suggest that you find a creative way for service providers to concisely present to your staff. In large schools, you might consider setting up stations that staff circulates through in small groups. Teachers have the written material and can make notes for themselves as they circulate or listen.

All of this information is available on Template 6: Organizing Information About Related Services. Although the principal would need to list the services categorically (i.e., Tutoring, English as a Second Language, Special Education, etc.), the actual cutting and pasting of the information is a clerical task that can be easily delegated for annual updating.

Helping Parents and Students Access Support Services

Parents have watched their students' experiences in school for years. Some parents are actively involved in working with their children and school, whereas others are not. Some of those in the latter category do not know what to do to support their children. Others did not have good experiences in their own schooling and probably are not surprised that their children are struggling. Another group of those parents are overwhelmed and are in a survival mode to support families. There are a myriad of reasons that some parents are not active and involved in their children's schooling. We often get "stuck" in trying to ferret out reasons for absent parents. Instead of spending time trying to find the "why's" of parent attitudes or behavior, investing time in directly supporting students in learning and working with parents to gain their confidence and cooperation will pay dividends.

Parents, regardless of their level of involvement, have some commonalities:

- They want the best for their children.
- They want to see their children be "successful."
- They do not like surprises, such as poor grades.
- They like to hear good news.

The most common complaint you will hear from parents of struggling students is: "Why didn't someone tell me sooner?"

The most common complaint you will hear from teachers is: "I can't get in touch with this parent," or "All they do is ask me what *I* am going to do about it."

The "Blame Game" gets us nowhere in terms of helping children learn. It is important that principals let parents and teachers hear the same, consistent message: "We are all in this together. Parents and teachers are all on the same side; we want to see our students and your children learn and grow. How can we do this together?"

Starting the school year by providing parents with all of the information and procedures for accessing help for their children will set the tone that we are "in this together." Information and user-friendly reference material about support services must be provided to all parents and students.

Again, do not expect that you can distribute this information in a newsletter and that everyone will be informed, able to communicate with staff at the school effectively, and access help when it is needed. Some steps to follow to support parent understanding and ability to transfer that to action are listed for you.

Informing Parents of Related Services

♦ Using the information you have compiled from *Organizing Information About Related Services*, create a quality brochure or handout that includes:

- Contact information for the school and special service providers
  - Office
  - Counseling, Attendance, Nurse
- Communication options for parents with the school
  - Parent Internet options
  - Phone calls to teachers with best times to call
  - Conference dates
  - Homework hotlines
- Communications that the school must expect from parents
  - Calls for absences
  - Signed progress reports
- School schedule and calendar
  - Daily schedule
  - School year calendar
  - Finals schedule
- Support services information
  - Descriptions by category

- Procedures for contacts
- Contact information
  - Positive messages that promote mutual support between family and school

An example of a Parent Information Summary (Template 5, page 60) is included for you. The school's daily schedule and the calendar should also be incorporated

♦ Develop a creative presentation summarizing the information above to include at open house or in an orientation with all parents.

- This can be done as part of an opening assembly with all parents.

- If parents are going to spend time in classrooms, the information can be shared by service providers in classrooms.

- At the secondary level, as parents go from class to class throughout the evening, the presentation can be made during the simulated lunch period.

♦ Distribute the informational brochure or handout materials that you have developed to the parents following the presentation.

- Make certain that you have prepared these materials so that they will be easy to store and easy to use.

- A magnet with commonly used school phone numbers is very well received by parents. If you can, leave room for parents to write teachers' phone numbers on the magnet. You can also provide blank magnets with the school name and mascot. That allows parents to write the numbers they use in ink on the magnet.

♦ Condense the information that you distributed and include it in your next newsletter for parents who were absent.

♦ Keep a supply of the brochures in the front office to give to the parents of new students throughout the year.

Assuring That Students Get the Help They Need in Time—On Time

Principals, teachers, and parents all are concerned that appropriate assistance be readily available for students *as* they need it. That implies that schools have systems in place to identify student needs, processes in place to facilitate placements, and intervention options available. Procedures for quickly identifying students needing support services should be refined and updated annually.

1. Use Student Intervention Matrix (Template 6 on page 62) to identify:

    -   How students who may require additional support or service are identified

    -   Procedures that are to be followed

    -   Actions that are to be taken

2. Schools often use a pyramid model to detail student intervention options. The pyramid model represents the number of students requiring service decreases as the intervention intensity increases. Although a pyramid is a useful model, use any design you are comfortable with to list current intervention options and the student population each serves. A Pyramid of Reading Instruction and Interventions, created by Vince Puzick, Literacy Resource Teacher at Palmer High School in Colorado Springs, Colorado, is included as a sample for you on page 64. Principals and schools using this model will have many pyramids: one for reading interventions, one for math interventions, and one for behavioral interventions, etc. It is a tool that is very useful in explanations to staff, parents, and students.

3. With a representative group of service providers, review all options and procedures.

    -   Identify what is working well.

    -   Identify what is not working.

    -   Problem solve: Identify the smallest change that will create the greatest improvement. A complete overhaul is rarely necessary.

    -   Identify any information about interventions or procedures that teachers will need.

    -   Develop a plan of action to distribute and explain the information to those who need it. That may include parents.

This process may take you all of your first school year. That is to be expected and will allow you to see how things are presently operating. It also will raise awareness levels of all involved about formal and informal processes that they use. Teachers, counselors, educational assistants, and others will see gaps that allow students to "fall through the cracks" and will be able to work together to refine processes and procedures. Additionally, the materials that you publish to parents and staff can be updated for next year in a timely way.

Template 5. Parent Information Summary (Example)

Challenger School
3333 Explorer Way
Anytown, USA 11111

School and Home Working Together

We have compiled this list of resources to help you know how to access services and information for your child at Challenger School. Some spaces have been left for you to fill in at Open House as you meet with your student's teachers. Keep this handy guide on your refrigerator at home with the magnet clip we have given you. We hope that this will be a ready reference for you as we work together to support your student's learning and performance this year. Together we can make a difference!

Resources for Help and Information

Office Receptionist	333-4444
Attendance Office	333-4445
Counseling Office	333-4446

Website: www.challengereagles@d-111.org

Personal Resources for My Student

Teacher/Staff	Number	Best Time to Call

Support Services

Academic Intervention Program Office	333-4447
Cafeteria	333-4451
Deaf Education Program	333-4448
English as a Second Language Office	333-4449
Extended School Year Programs	333-4450
Homework Hotline	333-4451
Tutoring Program Office	333-4452

Conference Dates and Times

Open House: September 10	7–9 PM
Parent Student Conferences:	
October 26	5 PM–9 PM
October 27	8 AM–4 PM
January 5	8 AM–4 PM
March 16	8 AM–4 PM

There will be no classes for students on conference days.

Progress Reports and Report Cards

Progress Reports will be sent home with students every two weeks on Fridays. Progress Reports are also available online through the Parent Link. During Open House, you will be given your password.

Parent Link Directions:

Go to website

Click on Parent Link

Enter your password

My Password:

You are also able to access your student's daily attendance records through Parent Link!

Report Cards will be distributed to you for Quarters 1, 2, and 3 during conferences and will be mailed the first week of June.

Template for Organizing Information About Related Services can be found at www.eyeoneducation.com and on the following page (61).

Template 5. Parent Information Summary

_____ School
Street Address
City, State, Zip

School and Home Working Together

We have compiled this list of resources to help you know how to access services and information for your child at Challenger School. Some spaces have been left for you to fill in at Open House as you meet with your student's teachers. Keep this handy guide on your refrigerator at home with the magnet clip we have given you. We hope that this will be a ready reference for you as we work together to support your student's learning and performance this year. Together we can make a difference!

Resources for Help and Information

Office Receptionist

Attendance Office

Counseling Office

Website:

Conference Dates and Times

Open House:

Parent Student Conferences:

Personal Resources for My Student

Teacher/Staff	Number	Best Time to Call

There will be no classes for students on conference days.

Progress Reports and Report Cards

Support Services

Academic Intervention Program Office

Cafeteria

Deaf Education Program

English as a Second Language Office

Extended School Year Programs

Homework Hotline

Tutoring Program Office

Parent Link Directions:

Go to

Click on Parent Link

Enter your password

My Password:

Template 6. Student Intervention Matrix (Example)

Identifying Student Needs	Procedures	Actions Taken
New Students:		
1. Diagnostic testing prior to placement in classes	Results are given to counselors for enrollment meeting with family.	• Students are placed in appropriate classes. • Counselors also interview parents about history and services needed. • Appropriate information is forwarded to service providers.
2. Study of school records from previous school	Materials given to appropriate service provider.	• A needs meeting is scheduled with the family. • Appropriate procedures are followed for identification of needed continuing services and placement.
Continuing Students:		
1. Teachers identify students who are struggling.	Teacher contacts literacy coach.	• Literacy Coach and teacher create modified materials/practices for in-class use.
2. Students on Individual Literacy Plans are identified for teachers.	Literacy coach meets with each teacher.	• Plans are reviewed and implications defined and translated to practice. • Placements are made in any needed intervention programs.
Students Moving to Next Level of Schooling:		
1. Special Education Coordinator establishes review staffing calendar with next school in April.	Review staffings are conducted with providers from both schools and families.	• Plans are developed collaboratively to assure provision of necessary services, programs, and classes at the in-taking school.

Template of the Student Intervention Matrix be found at www.eyeoneducation.com and on the following page.

Template 6. Student Intervention Matrix

Identifying Student Needs	Procedures	Actions Taken
New Students:		
1.		
2.		
Continuing Students:		
1.		
2.		
Students Moving to Next Level of Schooling:		
1.		

Pyramid of Interventions

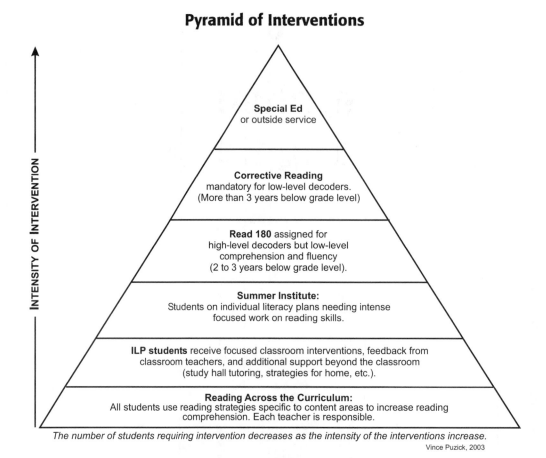

The number of students requiring intervention decreases as the intensity of the interventions increase.

Vince Puzick, 2003

Chapter Summary

In order to ensure that the related services are focused and responsive to learning problems and that they are based on thorough assessments that demonstrate student needs, you have examined your school's practices with several points in mind. First, you have identified the related services provided in your building, identified the professionals who deliver those services, and created a description of the students receiving that support. You have analyzed the data regarding those related services: How do they impact Adequate Yearly Progress? Are they included in the School Improvement Plan? How will you monitor their impact on student achievement? Of course, it is important that you inform staff, students, and parents of these related services and how to access them. You have created communications that keep staff informed of how to take advantage of these resources. In addition, parents are informed of the related services available to their children through presentations, newsletters, brochures, and other communications. All of your work is aimed at assuring that students get the help they need—on time—to increase their achievement. Are there tasks you need to tend to that will assure that Related Services are provided for your students? Better find that Entry Planner!

6
Accomplishment: Mobilizing Resources

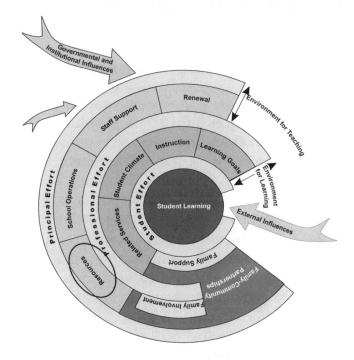

Essential Tasks

Identifying External Resources

Setting the Stage to Maximize Resource Use and Impact

Developing Relationships with External Resources and Contacts

Updating Staff

Informing Community Partners and Volunteers of School Information and Procedures

Accessing the Media as a Resource

6

Mobilizing Resources

Identifying, Developing, and Coordinating Resources

Identifying External Resources

We depend on external support to increase the capacity of the school's teaching and learning. External resources include school volunteers, community partnerships, programs for students and teachers, and sources of external funding. Naturally, community partners are concerned when there is a change in leadership. They wonder if operations will change. They are anxious to see if the new principal sees value in their contributions. The concern they feel will not be diffused until they meet you and begin developing a relationship with you.

It is important for you to identify external resources and support systems right away. In most cases, this will allow you to make initial contacts and to begin building relationships that will serve the school well. In fact, the sooner you begin to do this, the stronger the positive message will be that you value these people and programs.

Setting the Stage to Maximize Resource Use and Impact

For folks outside of the school—parents, community members, local businesses and organizations—who volunteer their time and resources, there is nothing more frustrating than offering and then not being utilized or appreciated.

It is important, too, to assure that staff involved with community partners understand the scope of the resources available, any parameters that must be followed, and any constraints involved. This does not have to be a time-consuming task.

In the annual start-up of schools, it is important to inform all stakeholders of the resources and then keep them informed throughout the school year. Annual updates at the beginning of each year will serve both new and current staff in better accessing and capitalizing on resources available to meet the needs of students in the school. Of course, information and user-friendly reference material about available resources should be accessible to staff throughout the year. For staff members involved with specific grant-funded projects, schedule necessary meetings during the first few weeks of the school year. In addition, information about the school and school procedures that impact the community partners must be communicated to them. Of increasing importance, media procedures must be communicated and understood by the staff.

Developing Relationships With External Resources and Contacts

We recommend that you take steps to identify all external resources that support your school and develop strategies to build relationships with these partners as soon as possible. Some strategies that you might consider include the following.

Identifying External Resources and Contacts

Template 7 (page 69) and Template 8 (page 71) are available to download from the website noted below Template 7. We recommend that you download the templates onto your computer or to your secretary's computer so that you can keep this information current and accessible. Key sources to start with as you compile this information are your secretary, your supervisor, lead teachers, and possibly the past principal.

Template 7. External Resources and Contacts: Businesses and Organizations (Example)

Business/ Organization	Contact Name & Address	Phone	E-mail	Other Number(s)	Service to School
Ex: Junior Achievement (JA)	Mr. Jerry Hoffman Junior Achievement 3333 JA Way Colorado Springs, CO 80909	719-111-2222	jhoff@ja.org	Fax: Cell:	Organizes employees of JA to teach units in sixth-grade classes

Template for External Resources and Contacts may be found at www.eyeoneducation.com and on the following page.

Template 7. External Resources and Contacts: Businesses and Organizations

Business/ Organization	Contact Name & Address	Phone	E-mail	Other Number(s)	Service to School
				Fax: Cell:	

Template 8. Community Partnerships—Volunteers (Example)

Relationship to School	Name & Address	Phone	E-Mail	Other Number(s)	Service to School
Parent	Julie Smith 2222 Parent Ave City, ST 80907	719-222-1111	jsmith@aol.com	Cell:	Assists with hearing and vision screening each year
Hillside Community Center					Provides room in the center for afternoon tutoring

Template for External Resources and Contacts may be found at www.eyeoneducation.com and on the following page.

Template 8. Community Partnerships—Volunteers

Relationship to School	Name & Address	Phone	E-Mail	Other Number(s)	Service to School

Strategies for Relationship Building

◆ Personal phone calls

Once the list of external resources is complete, it is important for you to initiate contact with each partner. If you are able to do this over the summer or very early in the year, you will be sending a clear message that you value and appreciate community partnerships. Although making a phone call to each partner may seem like a big time commitment, you will be amazed at the outcome. During the brief call:

• Introduce yourself

• Let the partner know that you are very interested in hearing their views on the school, that you want to learn about their involvement, and that you want to know what you can do to support them. Then, *listen…listen…listen…OR*

• You may prefer simply to set a time to meet with the partner and to have this discussion. If that is your preference, set up the meeting at the partner's establishment unless she/he prefers to come to the school. By going to the partner, you convey the message that her/his time is important to you and that you value her/him.

◆ Letter of Introduction

A less personal, but more time-effective, contact is a letter of introduction printed on school stationary. You will be giving the same messages as those identified in the phone call section. However, you also need to be clear about a next step in meeting with each of the partners. See Template 9 (page 73) for a sample letter.

Template 9. Letter of Introduction to Community Partners

Dear   ,

I am so excited to have been appointed to XYZ School as principal! One of the first items on my "to do" list is to make contact with those in the community who support our school and continue to make such a positive difference for our students, our staff, our school, and our school community. I have always believed that those of us working in the schools simply cannot make the difference for students alone. The efforts of those in the community who understand that children and their learning are essential for our community's healthy longevity are valuable resources.

You have worked with our school over time. I value your help and your insight about our school, its needs, and our future work together. I have a great deal to learn from you! I would also like to introduce myself to you, spend time getting to know you better, and make plans for our continued work together on behalf of the students at our school. I have (select one for your letter, or add an idea of your own)

- set aside the next week to meet individually with our community partners. My secretary, Mrs. Judy, will be following up with you to set a time for our meeting. I will be happy to meet with you at your place of business or at the school. The choice is yours. If next week will not work for you, please let Mrs. Judy know what date would be better.

- arranged for a morning coffee reception for all of our community partners. I so hope that you can attend. We will be meeting on Wednesday, August ___ from 8 AM until 9:30 AM in the library. Although many will be attending, I hope to spend individual time with each community partner. With that as a beginning, I look forward to spending more time with you as the year moves on.

- arranged for an afternoon focus session for all of our community partners. I hope that you can attend! We will be meeting on Wednesday, August ___ from 2:30 until 4:00 PM in the library. I am so looking forward to hearing your ideas about our school and your involvement here.

Until then, I will be working diligently to assure a smooth and productive start to the school year for our school community. If at any time you would like to talk to me, please feel free to call me at the number listed below or to e-mail me. If I am not immediately available, I will call you back just as quickly as I can. I am looking forward to seeing you soon!

With warm regards,

Template for the Letter of Introduction to Community Partners can be found at www.eyeoneducation.com for your modification.

- ◆ Community Partners Reception

  A time-effective way to meet all of your community partners is to host a reception for them. This is a good "next step" if you sent a letter of introduction. Your letter could include an invitation to this event. Receptions can follow all sorts of formats.

  - Morning coffees and mid to late afternoon time frames seem to be the best attended.

  - During the reception, be sure to include in your welcoming remarks your appreciation for the work these people do.

  - Social receptions allow you to circulate and meet people.

  - An open forum reception can allow you to raise topics and solicit partner feedback.

- ◆ Meeting with Your Community Partners

  Individual meetings with your community partners can be an excellent way to begin building relationships that can support your work and the school. Again, be sure to offer to come to their place of business to meet. Some may prefer to come to the school.

  During your meetings, calls, or contacts with your community partners, be certain to ask them to identify school needs and to help you find avenues to meet those needs. Do not ask people for "needs" or "problems" unless you also ask them for their ideas. To ask for the former without the latter is to ask people to set all of the problems on your shoulders alone. Remember to always give clear messages that "we are in this together."

We would offer one caution here. Be careful about making commitments that will require staff to commit time without first discussing it with the staff involved.

Updating Staff

Staff members need to have a working understanding of all resources and services available beyond their classrooms. An overview, with materials for ongoing reference, usually is enough for the majority of the staff. Those staff members directly connected with community partners' efforts will require more in-depth information.

Steps to Follow

Develop a document entitled *School Information and Procedures for Community Partners and Volunteers* for the staff packet. Staff members need to be aware of available resources, legalities and policies governing volunteer presence in the school, and volunteer interactions with children.

1. Use the information you had compiled by using the tools mentioned earlier:

   - Template 7. External Resources and Contacts: Businesses and Organizations (page 68)

   - Template 8. Community Partnerships—Volunteers (page 70)

   Condense the information to include the name of the business or organization, the service offered, and the procedure you have developed for *streamlining communication* and scheduling with each business/organization. Be thoughtful about your procedures for contacting the volunteers. If every staff member makes her/his own contact, volunteers can be overwhelmed with competing requests. See Template 10 (page 77) for a sample document.

2. Identify a strategy to remind all staff of the district's and school's policies, regulations, and practices related to media requests, interviews, and articles. Taking care of this during start-up of the school year will prevent situations that could result in mixed messages to media representatives or negative press.

3. This packet can be distributed to staff during a staff meeting early in the year with a concise overview, highlighting critical issues only. Working with the media is particularly critical.

4. **Grant-funded projects:** Using the information from *External Funding: Grant/Benefits/Gifts* (Template 11, page 79), schedule meetings with each group of staff who is responsible for a grant. These meetings typically will last for one hour. A productive grant meeting will:

   - Describe your understanding of the grant by giving an overview to the group.

   - Ask the group to boost your understanding by adding to your overview or correcting any information that is mistaken.

   - Review timelines, tasks, and monitoring procedures.
     - If there are no monitoring procedures written into the grant, develop them with the group.

- It is important that the group monitor progress throughout the year so that all involved can make mid-course corrections if needed to get the results you have identified.

- Establish a regular meeting schedule, usually quarterly. Develop a template agenda for your meetings. For example:

  - Progress report from participants, based on monitoring plan results

  - Identification of any problems or issues

  - Problem-solving session

  - Detail any changes, tasks, or responsibilities in writing for all team members

  - Set next meeting date

Template 10. School Information and Procedures
for Community Partners and Volunteers (Example)

Explorer School

2345 Navigator Way
Anytown, USA

Businesses and Organizations

The following businesses and organizations donate their time and service to our teachers and students. We appreciate their time and expertise in supporting our students! Each is listed with a description of the special volunteer service they contribute. **To contact them, please work through the Counseling Secretary, Judy Clark.** She will coordinate contacts so that the business partners are not overwhelmed with competing requests for help.

Parent Volunteers

We are fortunate to have parents who are active and involved in our school. To access help from parent volunteers, please contact our Parent Volunteer Chairman, Mrs. Becky Green, via e-mail at beckygreen@hotmail. com. She usually is able to respond to requests within 48 hours.

General Guidelines for Volunteers

- All of our volunteers must be registered with the school and district in order to work in our schools. If you have someone who wants to volunteer, please contact my secretary, Gladys Good.
- All volunteers have name tags that they wear while volunteering in the school. They either say "Volunteer" or are personalized, depending on the frequency of their involvement in the school.
- Adults in our building without name tags should be approached courteously and escorted to the office to check in and to receive a name tag.

Business/Organization	Service to School
Example: Junior Achievement (JA)	Organizes employees of JA to teach units in ninth-grade Civics classes

Template for School Information and Procedures for Community Partners and Volunteers can be found at www.eyeoneducation.com and on page 78.

Template 10. School Information and Procedures for Community Partners and Volunteers

_____ School

Street Address
City, State, Zipcode

Businesses and Organizations   **Parent Volunteers**

General Guidelines for Volunteers

-

-

-

Business/Organization	Service to School

Template 11. External Funding: Grants/Benefits/Gifts (Example)

School Year:

Program Title	Duration	Funding Amount	Organization Contact	Building Contact	Students Involved	Staff Involved
Ex: Breakfast Program Federal Program	Ongoing based on free/reduced lunch percentage	N/A	Central Office of External Funding 719-333-4444	Kitchen Manager: Mrs. Cleaver	Free to students qualifying for free/reduced services	Kitchen staff Administration
Ex: Title VI Federal Grant	One year evaluation due May 1	$20,000	Central Office of External Funding	Principal and Chair of Staff Development Committee: Mr. Jones	N/A	Staff Development Committee Benefit to all staff

Template for External Funding: Grants/Benefits/Gifts can be found at www.eyeoneducation.com and on page 80.

Template 11. External Funding: Grants/Benefits/Gifts

School Year:

Program Title	Duration	Funding Amount	Organization Contact	Building Contact	Students Involved	Staff Involved

Informing Community Partners and Volunteers about School Information and Procedures

In this day and age of increased security, it is very important that the principal be aware of and implement all district regulations related to non–staff members working in the school. Additionally, staff members who must enforce these practices need to know what to do and how to do it. Community partners need to know and use these practices and to understand the reasons for them.

Steps to Follow

1. Research all district policies and regulations related to having non-staff members in the building.

2. Develop a list of procedures for community partners to follow while in the school. These procedures are based on policy and implement regulations. For example:

   - *Policy* will speak to student safety and making certain that all adults in the building are licensed or approved by the district.

   - *Regulations* will provide steps to follow to have volunteers register with the district.

   - *School procedure list* should incorporate the registration steps and a sign-in practice so that the office is aware of who is in the building at any given time.

   Meet in a group with any office personnel who need to implement the procedures (e.g., the school secretary who will have a sign-in sheet for all visitors and volunteers.). Make any modifications in the procedures based on your conversation with office personnel.

3. Ask office personnel to make creative name badges for all community partners or volunteers to wear when they are in the building. If you have longstanding volunteers who are in the building repeatedly, you can make badges for them by name instead of "Community Volunteer." Being valued, even in simple ways, often can boost involvement and commitment.

4. Create a concise reference and informational sheet for your community partners. Make certain that it is an understandable document that is free of grammatical errors. It could include:

   - Name of school

   - Mascot

   - Mission statement

- Brief description of the school, including any school goals, motto, or statements demonstrating the value that the school places on partnerships that support students' learning

- Procedures for volunteers to follow while in the school. Introduce the procedure section with a brief statement that provides rationale for the procedures. These statements usually can be found in district policy documents.

5. Provide this document to all community partners and school volunteers. Strategies for distributing this document are listed below. Your time availability likely will dictate which option you elect to use:

    - The document can be mailed with a cover letter that explains the document and thanks them for their involvement.

    - The principal can schedule a welcome reception with light snacks to thank people, distribute the document, have the partners and volunteers tour the school, and build relationships.

    - The principal or a delegate can meet individually with every volunteer during her/his first visit to the school.

6. A copy of this document should be attached to the staff packet for their information. See *Updating Staff* on page 74.

Accessing the Media as a Resource

The term *media* can strike fear into the heart of any principal. We all have read articles and opinion columns and seen television news that report negative public school events and issues. We would encourage you, however, to consider this: **You can strategically build a network of media support that can be a strong resource for your school!**

The media can be a wonderful resource for your school. It is important that you communicate with your staff so that they are aware of procedures, regulations, and policy related to media practices in your school and district. Building this understanding throughout your staff will result in clear lines of communication with the media. These procedures will minimize the possibility of mixed messages to the media and adverse publicity. Once there is a problem with the media, the principal deals with the repercussions for weeks or longer, rebuilding relationships and refining procedures. It is best to avoid crises that require you to drop the ball on other important tasks you have in order to react to the crisis.

We recommend that you take the following action steps:

1. Know your district's policies and procedures related to media contacts.

- Who is the "point person" in your district for giving and receiving information with media personnel?
- What guidelines does your district/supervisor have for your communication with the media?
- Ask your district for a list of all media contacts for your reference.
- Always abide by your District's parameters.

2. Make contact with media contacts (seek approval of your supervisor).

- Make a phone call or send a letter introducing yourself as the principal of your school. Seek information about deadlines for submissions, contacts for presenters in classes, and programs that are available through the media for your school.

3. Routinely invite media personnel to school special events.

- Be sure to invite the appropriate media personnel for the purpose of the event.

General Guidelines for Working With the Media

♦ Always be honest with the media. If you are not, they will not believe you next time.

♦ Focus your conversations on the mission of the school. If asked questions about the school, answer them and bring the conversation back to how the issue relates to the school's mission.

- Example: A fire in the school. Reporter: "Aren't your students afraid about the safety of the school?" Answer: "Safety is always a priority for all of our school community. We have already taken steps to identify the cause and to evaluate any changes we might need to make. We have also taken steps to share classroom space to make certain that student learning will not be impacted because of the damage. We will keep you apprised of our progress."
- Assure the privacy of your students and staff.
- If photos are going to be used, make certain that appropriate permissions are completed.
- If interviews with students are involved, parental permission is a must. Make certain that no interviews take place on your campus without your direct knowledge. Do not allow students to be pulled from classes for interviews of any kind.

♦ Keep all media informed of new programs and special projects.

- Follow district procedures for news releases.

- Meet appropriate media deadlines.

- Remember that the format and appearance of your releases are very important.

♦ Partner with media personalities.

- Invite them to speak in classes.

- Utilize appropriate programs available through the media.

- If media has education columns or spots, volunteer to develop one. Assure that the product is top notch. Your product reflects on you and the school.

♦ Prepare for interviews. Practice.

♦ Always assume that your remarks are "on the record."

Communicating Media Procedures to Your Staff

Steps to Follow

1. Develop a guide for your staff with regard to working with the media. The content of this guide could include:

   - A concise statement about the purpose of the document and procedures. This typically can be found in district policy statements.

   - School procedures to use in working with the media that are based on district policy, regulations, and your supervisor's input.

     ▪ The list should include a school "point person." This person is the first to be notified if the media seeks information from the school and usually is the principal.

   - Hints and tips; feel free to use any of the tips listed in this chapter.

2. Distribute this guide to all staff members. This can be done in a large group setting. A concise summary and a Question & Answer session will be 30 minutes or less that is well invested!

Chapter Summary

In order to ensure that external communications meet the academic needs and programs in your building, you have carefully moved through a series of steps. First, you have identified the external resources and support systems. You then want to move quickly to build meaningful relationships with those resources: Make phone calls, send a letter of introduction, have a reception, and meet with those community partners who can impact your student body. It is important to update the staff, too, regarding all the resources available to them beyond the school's walls. In addition, it is crucial that principals communicate the policies and procedures for volunteer work in their building; staff members and community volunteers must know the procedures for external resources used in the building. Finally, you can use the media as a beneficial resource for your building. You must, however, be proactive and strategic in building a positive and productive relationship with the media. There are many important tasks associated with *Mobilizing Resources* to benefit student learning in your school that you will want to note on your Entry Planner.

7

Accomplishment: Organizing and Supporting School Operations

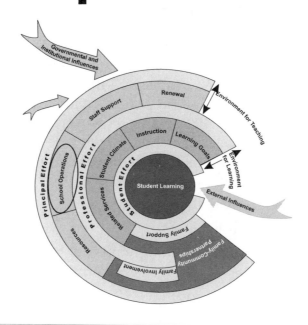

Essential Tasks

Knowing Your Facility

Developing a Positive and Productive Partnership with Your School Secretary

Reviewing Operational Systems

Hiring Great Teachers

Hiring Great Classified Staff Members

7

Organizing and Supporting School Operations

Designing Systems to Efficiently and Effectively Impact Student Learning

Know Your Facility

To become informed about your facility, first get acquainted with your custodial and maintenance staff. Draw on their expertise and experience to help you familiarize yourself with the facility. Enlist building maintenance staff to conduct a "walk-through" of the building(s) and grounds with you to review the systems for heating, cooling, ventilation, lighting, water, safety, and security. This review of buildings and grounds serves two important purposes. It informs your knowledge of the facility. But equally important, it provides a venue for sending important messages to support staff:

- You are a valued member of the school team.
- The work you do is very important.
- I am interested in you, as a person, and in your perspectives and opinions, to further increase our school's performance.
- I am here to support your success.

Once you have familiarized yourself with the building and grounds and the significant facility systems, we suggest that you:

- Gain knowledge of the security systems and procedures related to alarms and keys.
- Ensure that the building is ready for the return of staff and students.
- Learn the systems for maintenance and safety work orders.
- Review procedures for groups using the building.

Becoming Familiar With Security Systems

Many principals report that the reality of the job hits them when they are handed the keys to the building. As soon as possible, learn the building security systems. First, become familiar with the alarm procedures to determine:

1. How do I set and disable alarms?

2. What are the procedures when the alarm sounds?

3. What do I do if the alarm is accidentally tripped? (a noted hazard for beginning principals!)

Inquire about the procedures for secure access for building keys to learn:

4. Who has keys for various areas of the building?

5. Did staff turn in keys for the summer?

6. If so, what are procedures for efficiently distributing keys when staff return?

Ensuring the Readiness of the Building

A clean and well-maintained building is critical to ensuring a smooth start to the school year. Meet with custodial staff and inquire about the summer work schedule, work orders, and functioning of safety systems. Work with your custodial staff to inquire:

♦ Is summer work on schedule? If not, determine what is needed to ensure that the building is ready for staff and students. If the building will not be ready, be sure to contact your immediate supervisor to discuss options.

♦ Have work orders for repairs and materials requests been completed? If not, are they scheduled for completion?

♦ Are required safety systems and handicap access features functioning?

Getting Acquainted With Procedures for Requesting Maintenance Work

Gain an understanding of the basic systems in place for requesting, tracking, and completing work orders in the building and at the district level. Review the current formal and informal systems for maintenance requests within the building:

♦ How do staff members report maintenance needs or safety concerns?

♦ How are maintenance requests and safety updates tracked for efficient completion?

♦ How do maintenance personnel communicate with the principal?

Acquaint yourself with district processes for requests from the District Maintenance Department:

- ♦ Who are the key contacts for central services?
- ♦ How are work orders for maintenance or safety concerns initiated?
- ♦ What is the process for tracking progress of maintenance work?
- ♦ Sample work order or tracking system form

Reviewing Policies and Procedures for Groups Using the Facility

External groups often use school facilities throughout the year. Ensure "user-friendly" practices by maintaining effective systems for requesting, scheduling, and monitoring facility use. First, work with appropriate custodial staff to review the district policies and current building systems. Are effective processes in place to:

- ♦ Submit building use requests?
- ♦ Maintain a chronological record of building use requests and decisions (approved or denied)?
- ♦ Provide an effective calendar/schedule that prevents scheduling conflicts?
- ♦ Inform night custodians of building use and need to open the building?
- ♦ Alert custodians if changes are made to the building use schedule?

Revisiting the Status of Your School Facility

Once the school year has begun, conduct a repeat walk-through and a follow-up debriefing with your custodian now that school is in session. Review with her/him any needs that have been communicated by staff. Do all of the classrooms have desks, chairs, and necessary equipment? What is the appearance of the building and the grounds? Have all the boxes and materials been delivered to the appropriate locations? Have the temperatures in the various locations in the building been monitored? Has playground equipment been checked again for safety? Does the coordination and communication between the day and evening custodial staff lend itself to a smooth operation? Are the alarm systems in good working order, and do all staff members have easy access to the building at the times that they need it? Have there been any concerns regarding community groups who have been using the building after school hours? Is there anything that needs to be communicated to staff members that would be helpful to the custodial staff?

In your communication with your custodian, be sure to acknowledge the importance of her/his role in the smooth workings of the school and the impact of her/his performance on teaching and learning. Demonstrate both verbally and in writing your appreciation for all that was done to prepare for the new school year. If there are things that you perceive are not at a satisfactory level, now is a good time to talk about this. Clarity in terms of your expectations and an openness to problem solve with your custodian in order to get the desired results will contribute greatly in ensuring that the facility supports the important goals of the school.

Developing a Positive and Productive Partnership with Your School Secretary

The performance of your school secretary and the quality of your relationship with this person are vital to your success as a principal and to the smooth running of the school. When you work as a team, "tall buildings truly can be leaped," and when you have not taken the time to build a trusting and committed relationship with clear coordination, you often work against each other. Here are a few ideas for getting off on the right foot.

♦ Take the time to get to know your secretary. Bring in breakfast or lunch on one of the first days your secretary returns and begin to establish a relationship. Ask your secretary to tell you about herself/himself and her/his history with the district and the school. Use this as opportunity for your secretary to get to know you as well.

♦ Schedule regular times to meet, likely frequently during those first weeks on the job. Let your secretary inform you of general office routines and key things that you particularly need to be aware of so that you can make the back to school process go smoothly. Ask questions such as "What do I need to know or attend to that I may not be aware of? Are there things that you think I may not have thought about or need to be reminded of?"

♦ Design a time for you to meet to discuss priorities and work styles. What is most important to each of you and will allow both of you to perform your duties efficiently and with joy?

♦ In order for secretaries to be effective, it is important that they know your schedule and your whereabouts. Develop a routine time to review calendars.

♦ The school secretary and office personnel are most often the first people that staff members, parents, and visitors meet when they arrive at school. What are the messages you want them to receive from your school office (i.e., you are important, we are happy to see you, we are here to serve you, we are organized and informed, we are problem solvers and if we don't know the answer, we'll help you find it)? A discussion about how people are to be greeted, how the phone is to be answered, what materials should be easily available for distribution, and how the office looks and is organized is important in ensuring that the office climate is a source of pride for everyone.

♦ The role of school secretary can be all-consuming and very demanding. Ensure that trained coverage is available in order to allow your secretary necessary lunch and rest breaks.

♦ Design procedures for efficiency. How do you want the mail screened and organized? Different colored folders for signatures, budget items, district communications, immediate action, etc., can be very helpful. The use of a "tickler file" requesting your secretary to return certain materials to you on a specific date allows you to attend to matters in a timely way. The creation of a checklist to which you can easily designate routine tasks as materials cross your desk can be very efficient (e.g., forward to _____, make ___ copies, place in staff meeting agenda folder, etc.).

♦ Clarify your preferences on interruptions during times that you are involved in conferences, observations, and planning; under what conditions should you be contacted on your cell phone or pager? Return to these issues as necessary.

♦ Schedule monthly meetings (or more frequent, if necessary) to assess how things are going. What's working for each of you? What's not? What needs more clarification or coordination?

Be sure to regularly and routinely express your appreciation for all the support your secretary provides to you, the staff, the students, and the community. Public and private praise, feeling informed and "in the know," and demonstrations of personal concern are the three greatest motivators reported by employees. By building each of these behaviors into your relationship, you will contribute significantly to the morale and job performance of your secretary.

Reviewing Operational Systems

The School Office

Although the school office is always a busy place, it is often even more so during the first weeks of school. The phones are ringing, enrollment reports are due, student records are being sent and received, new students (and staff) are being oriented, and everyone wants it NOW! Recognizing the increased stress that your office staff is under, you will want to ensure that the structures in place are working. Check in with your school secretary regularly. What's working and what's not? What support does she/he need from you? Is there adequate personnel support during these first busy weeks?

Take the time to stand back and observe how parents, students, and staff members are served upon entering the office. Are they immediately greeted, or are they ignored until a task is finished? Does the greeting make them feel welcomed and valued? Is the issue or need that they are asking to be addressed handled in a helpful and efficient manner? If the question cannot be answered, is help offered in finding the answer or solving the problem?

How a person is treated upon entering the school can set the whole tone for one's day; am I encouraged or discouraged about how my day is going to go? Upon regular monitoring of the "office climate," provide feedback to your school secretary and office personnel. Again, assure them of their importance in realizing the mission of the school, demonstrate your appreciation for their talents and hard work, and let them know that you are here to support them. Determine if there are needs that you can address. Provide them feedback about the positive observations you have made in terms of "office climate" and clarify any expectations that are important to address.

Class Schedules

It will be very important to check the status of the class schedules. Have the schedules for the coming school year already been finalized? Have all staff members been informed of the schedules? If the schedules are all in place, you'll want to review them to ensure there are no errors or omissions. As you review the schedules, what parameters and priorities drove the schedule (blocks of time allocated for specific disciplines, common planning time for grade levels, departments, and teams, specific times that support an appropriate number of students in the lunchroom, on the playground, etc.)?

If schedules have not been designed or are incomplete, it is important that this becomes one of your top priorities, and it is equally important that you do not tackle this task in isolation. Class schedules have significant implications for effective instruction and staff morale. Enlist the advice and assistance of key personnel to provide guidance and insight. Ensure that schedules are communicated to all personnel prior to their reporting date, and, if you were responsible for its development, include a set of principles that guided the development of the schedule. Teachers have a strong, personal interest in the schedule; typically they will adjust to and accept changes if they are provided with a rationale and understand that changes were not made in an arbitrary or capricious manner.

Room Assignments

Have all personnel been assigned to classrooms, and has everyone received this communication? Again, if this task has been completed, look at a blueprint and take a tour of the building to determine the rationale for classroom assignments.

If room assignments are incomplete, again enlist the advice and assistance of key personnel to provide guidance and insight. Ensure that room assignments are communicated to all personnel, and, if you were responsible for making the assignments, include a set of principles that guided the development of the assignments. Additionally, if there are issues regarding overcrowding in your building, causing some teachers/programs not to have their own room, make a point to meet personally with these individuals, brainstorming with them the best support system that you can. Where can they store materials and valuables? What additional types of carts or supplies would help them? Obviously, you can't build them a room, but demonstrating concern and support for their situation and appreciation for their willingness to "make this work" will contribute greatly to their morale.

Class Size/Enrollment

Oftentimes, the district has a student-to-teacher ratio that guides class size. Make yourself aware of those guidelines and the procedures to follow once a maximum or minimum number of students is realized. Check pre-registration for "hot spots" to monitor, and ask your secretary or registrar to keep you informed of enrollment and class size status, particularly during the first few weeks of the school year.

Out of District/ Out of School Boundary Permits

You likely will receive requests for permits to attend your school from other districts or other schools in your district. Typically, districts have guidelines for approving and denying these requests with regard to both the time of the year the requests are considered and variables such as projected class size, special programming needs, transportation, etc. You will want to acquaint yourself with these guidelines and possibly speak with your supervisor regarding any additional guidance they might provide.

School Calendar

Again, you want to check the status of the school calendar. Has this already been developed, reviewed, and printed? Typically, there are two levels of school calendars: the external calendar that reflects all student-related dates (attendance dates, holidays, open house, school programs and assemblies, early dismissals for staff development, parent–teacher conferences, after-school programs, parent–teacher organization [PTO] meetings, etc.) and the internal calendar that reflects all staff-related dates (staff meetings, department/team meetings, district meetings, principal meetings out of the building, staff development programs, testing dates, standing committee meetings, after-school tutorials, etc.) Certainly, dates will be added to the calendar throughout the school year as needs arise, but as many dates as you can confirm and provide notice to your internal and external community, the better planning they all can do.

Staff Handbook

You will want to review the current staff handbook with several purposes in mind.

- ◆ First, to inform you of the requirements, procedures, and areas of importance that have been identified and followed to date,
- ◆ Second, to identify information or procedures that you may find confusing or that you don't understand,
- ◆ Third, to determine if there are any procedures that you find concerning and feel the need to be modified at this time, and
- ◆ Last, to identify any areas that may not be addressed in the current handbook that you feel are important and need to be included.

We caution you to not conduct a "major overhaul" on the staff handbook prior to this first school year. A staff handbook typically represents the stated norms of a building and reflect "how we do business here." Although you may find a number of areas that you hope to modify, unless they are most pressing, these changes will best be made following some time to observe the procedures and talk with staff members regarding the effectiveness of the present processes. And, of course, you'll need to check if you need to send handbooks (or certain pages containing changes) to be printed for distribution.

Any changes or additions that you do make you will want to bring to the attention of your staff during one of your beginning of the year meetings or orientation.

Reviewing the Ordering/ Receipt of Materials and Equipment

One of the biggest "energy boosters" for teachers is arriving at school to find the materials and equipment that they had ordered, there just waiting for them! It's kind of like "Christmas in August" seeing all their new supplies and materials, and it contributes to the excitement of beginning a new school year. On the other hand, one of the biggest "energy deflaters" is arriving at school and finding that their orders have not arrived or that no one knows where they are. As the principal, you can contribute greatly to the "holiday happiness" by meeting with your secretary and custodian (or whoever is responsible for orders and delivery locations) and checking the status of all orders. If calls need to be made regarding materials that have not arrived or to check on back orders, before the school year is the best time to do this. The two things that you want to ensure are that all ordered materials have arrived on time and that these materials are marked and in locations that are easily accessible to the teachers.

You may also want to check with your office personnel to see if there are supplies that the principal typically orders that may not have been completed by your predecessor (teacher plan books, attendance forms, discipline forms, registration materials, calendars, etc.). Great questions to continue to ask of your school secretary as you are preparing for the school year are "What haven't I done that I should be doing? What haven't I asked that I should be asking? What needs to be ready when?" Let your secretary know that you want and need her/his input and guidance as you acquaint yourself with your new responsibilities.

Reviewing the Budget

Although you may want to wait until you get the school year underway before you do a thorough analysis of the school budget, you certainly will want to get a general orientation from your school bookkeeper or secretary. Key areas that you will want to focus on are:

- ♦ What is the overall yearly budget amount?
- ♦ How is that budget determined?
- ♦ What is the balance of each line item? Are there any over-expenditures?
- ♦ What level of decentralization exists in the budget? In other words, do departments, teams, grade levels manage their own budget expenditures? What is my role in approving these expenditures?
- ♦ Are there any restrictions regarding the transfer of funds between one line item and another?

◆ What are budget issues that I should anticipate in the first two months on the job?

You likely will want to schedule a monthly budget review meeting with your bookkeeper or school secretary to be conducted throughout the school year in order to monitor expenditures and anticipate ordering timelines and policies regarding carryover funds.

You also will want to schedule a budget meeting with your district supervisor or the financial officer to clearly understand the expenditures that are addressed at the district level and the expenditures that are to be assumed at the building level. Additionally, you will want to know any restrictions regarding your budget and from whom you should seek approval if modifications are requested.

Transportation

The beginning of the school year is also the time to monitor how well everything is going transporting students to and from school. Is bus transportation running smoothly? Are drop-offs and pick-ups on time? Has the behavior requirements for students riding the bus been clearly communicated and practiced as well as consequences delineated? Are the staff members assigned to meet the buses routinely and promptly at the designated stops? Is there a clear procedure to follow when bus issues arise?

School bus drivers probably have one of the most responsible, yet under-appreciated and under-acknowledged, jobs in the school system. If you haven't had the opportunity to meet personally with each of them, now is the time to do so. Invite them into the school for a breakfast with you once they conclude their routes. Use this time to reinforce how important their role is to realizing your school's mission; thank them for their commitment to your school and students. Inquire if there are any pressing concerns at this time that you can help them address. Be sure to inform them of any special needs, physical or emotional, of students whom they transport. Arrange to have any special education teachers, the social worker, or the school nurse attend a part of this meeting if specific information needs to be shared. Very often, transportation problems can be prevented if information and proper training are provided up front.

In addition to monitoring the bus transportation, observe the traffic patterns in and out of the school parking lot. Are parents or student drivers complying with all of the safety regulations regarding speed, directionality, and unloading zones? Are students arriving at school or on the playground prior to supervision being provided? Are students leaving school grounds in a timely manner, or do follow-ups need to be made with parents and/or day care providers?

Food Services

"Food is fuel," and clearly students and teachers need fuel to carry out their important work. The food services employees provide a valuable service, and you will want to ensure that this service runs as smoothly as possible. Stopping in for a cup of coffee and meeting with the food services staff will go a long way to communicate the three key messages:

- ♦ You and the services you provide are important to our school.
- ♦ We appreciate your talent and hard work.
- ♦ I am here to support you doing your best work.

As you observe students entering and eating in the school cafeteria, consider the criteria that you would use when choosing to return to a restaurant that you've eaten in before. Were you greeted in a pleasant and welcoming manner? Were you served efficiently? Was the food at a quality that you enjoyed? Was the setting appealing and the noise level acceptable? Were the norms and expectations of the customers reasonable and consistently followed?

Work with your food services staff as well as the staff members assigned to monitor the cafeteria to create conditions conducive to everyone enjoying their breakfast and lunch times. Do the schedules work, or do they need to be adjusted? Are the expectations reasonable, and have they been communicated, demonstrated, and practiced? Do students and staff demonstrate mutual respect?

Hiring Great Teachers

One of the most important tasks you will ever do as a principal is the hiring of your staff. In the section on supervision and evaluation, we quote the research that strongly indicates that *teacher expertise is the single most important determinant of student achievement*. With that being the case, you *never* want to settle for an average or merely adequate educator. It will result in you spending valuable time in remediation (and possibly termination), and, in the process, your students and colleagues will be negatively impacted. In addition, the professionals whom a principal hires speaks volumes about the standards and expectations that the principal has for her/his teaching staff.

A common mistake that the writers of this manual have observed with beginning principals is that they may underestimate both the importance of staff selection and the time that is necessary for hiring top performers. Our advice is clear and strong: invest the time and skills necessary to find the finest employees you can possibly find. The investment will be returned to you and your school community a thousand fold.

Let us offer these additional suggestions before we move into the stages of the interview process:

- When reviewing the applicants from the district pool, if you find that you do not have a strong enough pool to select for interviews, request the personnel office to review the application files to ensure there aren't additional applications that haven't been given to you, or request that the position be re-advertised in order to build a stronger pool.

- After the interview process, if you still do not find a teacher or employee who meets your standards, speak with the personnel office about hiring a temporary person to serve in this position until you find the person who meets all of your qualifications.

Preparing for the Interview: "Begin With the End in Mind"

If you don't clearly know the qualities that you are looking for in a candidate, you may find that most anyone will do. What is it that your school stands for and that you are committed to providing your students and your community? To find these answers, review your school's mission and vision statements as well as the essential curriculum. In the book *Teachers Wanted, Attracting and Retaining Good Teachers* (2004), Daniel Heller suggests that you ask four key questions:

- What do we want students to know and be able to do? (curriculum)
- What methods do we use to help students achieve these goals? (pedagogy)
- How do we want students and teachers to act? (school and classroom climate)
- How should we treat teachers and students? (personal relationships)

You may find that the answers to these questions exist in your school documents, and it's a matter of drawing out the key information for the purpose of designing the interview questions. You may also find that this hasn't been clearly defined yet at your school. Although you will want to do this at a later time in collaboration with your staff, for your purposes now, these questions will serve as the pre-interview discussion with your interview committee.

Whereas in the past teachers typically were hired solely by the building principal, it now is commonplace for the principal to include staff members from the school as part of the selection committee. This is helpful for three reasons:

- You gain multiple perspectives in the selection process regarding both the qualifications of the applicants and the match to your school.
- The selection committee members are invested in the new employee's success.

◆ Candidates are provided with a microcosm of the staff they will be working with if they were to join your school team. This allows the candidates to "get a feel" for the working environment and relationships to see if it is a fit for them.

As valuable as it is to have staff members be a part of the hiring process, you must remember that teachers have not typically received training for staff selection. In order to do a good job, they need to both understand their role and the process that will be followed and have clear criteria for selection. To this end, you will want to address the following.

Suggested Roles and Process for Interviews

◆ The principal will conduct the paper screening and select candidates for interviews

◆ The interview committee will identify "key indicators or qualities" they are looking for, based on the four questions cited above, as well as possibly two others (Are there any unique aspects to our school or to this position that would warrant special skills or experience? Are there any unique characteristics of our team or department that would warrant special skills or experience?). Once the key indicators have been identified, the committee will select/develop questions that would solicit evidence of these indicators (see possible questions beginning on page 101).

◆ Following each interview, all participants will privately complete an evaluation sheet reflecting their impressions of the candidate. These will be referred to later during an intermittent or final discussion of all of the candidates.

◆ Every committee member, through turn taking, will have the opportunity to identify her/his top one to two candidates and her/his reasoning for these choices. Discussion will follow with the committee recommending the consideration of their top candidates to the principal.

◆ The principal will follow up with reference checks, getting back to the committee regarding the final selection decision and the rationale for the selection.

Note that this process has staff members highly engaged in determining the selection criteria, creating the questions, interacting with the candidates through the questioning and discussion, individually evaluating each candidate, and participating in a committee discussion to recommend top candidates for consideration. However, at the end of this collaborative process, it is the principal who needs to conduct the reference checks and make the final decision. This is because it is the principal who will serve as this employee's supervisor and evaluator. It is imperative, therefore, that the principal be comfortable with the decision that is made.

Possible Interview Questions

In selecting interview questions, you may want to consider those listed below. It is suggested that you select or create questions that reflect the key indicators and qualities that you are looking for in a candidate. Remember that the same set of questions needs to be asked of every candidate to ensure that all applicants have the same opportunity to present themselves.

Possible Interview Questions

Curriculum

1. What are the three most important skills or ideas all students should learn in the discipline of _____? Explain your rationale. (Heller, 2004)

2. What has been the most significant academic accomplishment by students in your classroom (or during your student teaching) this past year? To what do you attribute that accomplishment?

3. How do you keep yourself abreast of the most current research and instructional strategies? (Blaydes, 2004)

4. Describe your level of expertise with technology and share how you would utilize technology in your classroom. (Blaydes, 2004)

5. What opportunities, if any, have you had in serving on building or district curriculum committees or study groups? If you have had this experience, what important learnings have you derived from this experience?

6. What do you consider your academic areas of expertise? What experiences, education, and training served to develop this expertise?

7. What is your approach to planning to ensure that your instruction is aligned with the content standards and benchmarks?

8. How do you use assessment data to improve instruction and increase student learning?

Pedagogy/Management

9. Our school teaches in 2½-hour literacy blocks with students remaining in their homeroom. Describe the structure you might use for this instruction and how both direct and independent work would look.

10. What would you say is an optimal ratio of student to teacher talk in a class? (Heller, 2004)

11. How do you deal with the diversity of types of learners in a class? Give an example of differentiation that you have found successful. (Heller, 2004)

12. Who has had the most influence on your thinking and philosophy of education? (Heller, 2004)

13. What tools have you found to be most successful in assessing student progress in your classroom? (Blaydes, 2004)

14. There is much emphasis on writing today. Describe the steps of the writing process and how it would look in your classroom. (Blaydes, 2004)

15. You have seven students in your classroom who are more than a year behind in reading and writing. What interventions would you use or explore to try to ensure significant growth in their achievement?

16. An area that many of our children are challenged by is mathematics communication. If you found that was a significant deficit for students in your classroom, what interventions might you employ?

17. Briefly explain three methodologies for teaching _____. Have you found one more effective than the others? (Heller, 2004)

18. What approaches do you use to engage parents in effectively supporting their child's education?

School and Classroom Climate/Management

19. It is the third month of school and we are visiting your classroom during _____ class. Paint us a picture of a typical day. What are the students doing? What are you doing? What does the room environment look like?

20. What self-esteem building strategies do you find most effective in working with students? (Blaydes, 2004)

21. What are the steps you would take with a student whose acting-out behavior is escalating? (Heller, 2004)

22. What does respect look like between teachers and students? between students and students? between teachers and teachers? between teachers and parents? between teachers and administrators? (Heller, 2004)

23. A number of building and classroom discipline systems are used in schools. Have you received training in any particular system(s)? How would you describe your basic philosophy and approach to discipline?

24. What is your definition of "team"? What qualities or skills would you bring to a team of teachers that you might work with?

Personal Relationships/Personal Qualities

25. How do you feel when a student challenges your opinion or statement of fact? (Heller, 2004)

26. What three adjectives would your students use to describe you? your colleagues? your supervisor? (Blaydes, 2004)

27. How do you take care of yourself? (Heller, 2004)

28. Describe a time when you had a conflict with a colleague? How was it resolved? (Blaydes, 2004)

29. What was your greatest failure, and what did you do about it? (Heller, 2004)

30. What do you find the most challenging about teaching? the most rewarding?

31. What do you feel confident that you could contribute to the _____ school community?

32. You have begun teaching at our school and are confronting a situation that you really don't know how to handle. What would be your approach to finding a solution?

33. What do you hope to gain from working at _____ School?

34. What have you done that you are most proud of? (Heller, 2004)

Unique Aspects to School/Team/Department

35. _____ is a very diverse school community reflecting many different ethnic and cultural groups. As a teacher, what do you see as your role in honoring and celebrating this diversity? How have you demonstrated this in your past teaching experiences?

36. What has been your level of experience with special needs students in your classroom? What are the most important factors in ensuring that inclusion is successful?

37. _____ School has an adviser/advisee system in which every staff member is responsible for.... What qualities do you possess that would contribute to you being effective in this role?

38. Our team uses _____ (i.e., a critical friends process) to address common instructional issues and to do collaborative scoring of student work. What level of receptivity and/or experience would you bring in this area?

Checking References on Finalists

Most school districts require a minimum of two reference checks on each candidate prior to her/him being approved for hire. If this is not a district policy, this is something that you want to ensure that you do on your own. Past performance is a very strong indicator of future performance, and you can avoid costly mistakes by taking the time to conduct thorough and thoughtful reference checks with the immediate supervisor(s).

Questions That You May Want to Ask When Conducting a Reference Check

- What was the position/responsibilities of this candidate when she/he served in your school?
- What do you see as this persons' strengths?
- What did you identify as areas requiring growth or improvement?
- How was this person perceived by students? colleagues? parents?
- What was the greatest contribution that this person made while working in your school?
- What adjectives would you use to describe this person?
- On a scale from 1 to 10 (with 10 being the highest), what ranking would you give this person in each of the following areas:

___ Commitment	___ People skills	___ Instructional skills
___ Energy	___ Team player	___ Communication
___ Dependability	___ Discipline	___ Attendance
___ Judgment	___ Professional growth	___ Initiative
___ Love of children	___ Sense of Humor	___ Curricular Knowledge
___ Versatility		

- Is there any reason this candidate should not be supervising and/or working with children?
- Is there anything else that is important for me to know about this candidate?
- Would you re-hire this person, if given the opportunity, without any reservation?

When conducting reference checks, listen for what is *not* being said as well as what is being said. When being interviewed as a reference, some people are hesitant to give negative information, so rather than speak directly, they provide limited responses.

Hiring Great Classified Staff Members

In the section above, we focused on the hiring of your teaching staff, but we recognize, too, that you likely will have the responsibility of hiring classified staff members (custodians, secretarial and clerical staff, paraprofessionals, etc.). The selection of these staff members is no less important. Although they are not responsible for the direct instruction of your students, they greatly impact the environment and the conditions in which your teachers work. They have the power to positively or negatively affect the morale, climate, and efficiency of a building.

We recommend using a very similar process in selecting classified staff members as we did for the teaching staff:

♦ Ensure an adequate pool of strong candidates.

♦ "Begin with the end in mind." Identify what you want in a custodian, secretary, etc.

♦ Develop questions that will provide insight into each of those qualities.

♦ Conduct thorough reference checks, tailoring the questions from the sample above to reflect the position which you are filling.

In addition, we would add two more suggestions.

♦ For a position such as a custodian or building secretary, ask someone specialized in that area to be a part of the interview team. For example, a district supervisor of maintenance or a custodian from another building who enjoys a stellar reputation, or a building secretary from another building who possesses the qualities you are seeking. If you are interviewing for a paraprofessional position, be sure to include on the interview team the staff members with whom the paraprofessional will be working most closely.

♦ Do not hesitate to design and administer skill performance assessments that reflect the major tasks of the position (word processing, budget tasks, building safety procedures, etc.).

Substitute Teachers

You will want to ensure that the procedures for preparing for, procuring, and supporting substitute teachers in your building have been well designed and well communicated. Check the present procedures to determine if they are complete and ensure that all new staff members are informed. Does each teacher have the phone number and procedure for requesting a substitute and the guidelines for advance notice, if possible? Are lesson plans clearly written and accompanying manuals and materials easily accessible? Are backup materials available, if needed, to ensure students have beneficial work to do as time permits? Does each teacher have a substitute teacher folder that is easily accessible and visible in the classroom and that contains:

- Current class lists
- Seating charts
- Daily schedules
- Weekly notice of special events and activities
- Duty schedules

- School and classroom rules
- Discipline procedures
- "Buddy teacher" and some designated "student helpers" whom they can call on to ask any questions or help them address concerns?

Typically, an office person is designated to welcome substitute teachers, show them around the building, and accompany them to their classroom. Because great substitute teachers are such a valuable asset to the school, you will want to ensure that everyone does their part to make *your* school the school to which all the substitutes want to return.

Regular Monitoring of Staff Needs

The successful learning and positive behavior of your students is highly dependent on the skills and motivation of your staff. In turn, staff members are dependent on the attention given to the structures that support their work. It is very important throughout the school year, but particularly during this first month, that you monitor those structural needs regularly and carefully. Depending on the size and structure of your school, this monitoring may be done on an individual basis or via grade-level leaders, team or department chairpersons. However you design it, you will want to check in weekly for the first few weeks on key areas. We have provided an example (Template 12 on the following page) that you may want to consider using for monitoring key operations.

Additionally, another communication device that other principals have used, particularly in the first weeks of school and then possibly every other week after that, is just putting an index card in each staff member's mailbox on Thursdays. On one side of the card is printed "What's Working?" and on the other side of the card is printed "What's Not Working?". By asking staff members to turn in these cards to you by Friday, you have a quick status check from everyone and a start on next week's To Do list.

Template 12. Beginning of the Year Status Check

Starting the school year is challenging work, especially with a new principal on board. In wanting to ensure that the "basics" are covered to support you doing your best work, I'm asking that sometime each week for the first four weeks, you (as an individual, a team, a department) complete this form, providing a status check of how you are doing in each of these areas and informing me of any needs that you have. Thanks, in advance, for taking the time to keep me up to speed. Once I get your feedback, I'll follow up with you. Have a great week!

1 = Looks good! No problems!   2 = Need some minor assistance   3 = HELP in a big way!

Note: If you've got some 3s, don't hesitate to bypass the form and come on in to see me.

_____   1.   Class Size/Enrollment

Comments:

_____   2.   Schedules (Class, Specials, Lunch, etc.)

Comments:

_____   3.   Materials/Supplies/Equipment/Furniture

Comments:

_____   4.   Budget Items/Issues

Comments:

_____   5.   School Calendar

Comments:

_____   6.   Information we need to know....

Comments:

_____   7.   Student/Parent Concerns

Comments:

Template of the Beginning of the Year Status Check can be found at www.eyeon education.com.

When People Don't Do What You Expect Them to Do

Throughout this section, we have asked you to monitor the various operations and systems in your school. While conducting your observations and gathering data and feedback, it likely will become apparent that some members of your staff aren't doing what you expect them to do or aren't performing at the level at which you expect them to perform. This probably isn't much different than when you were in the classroom and had the opportunity to observe and gather data on your students. In the book *Why Employees Don't Do What They're Supposed to Do and What to Do About It* (1999), Fournies emphasizes that the key to addressing these issues constructively is determining *why* this is happening. By understanding why your expectations are not being met, you can design the appropriate response and solution.

Five reasons why people don't do what they are expected to do:

- They *don't know what* they're supposed to do
- They *don't know how* to do it
- They *don't want to* do it
- There are *roadblocks or constraints* (time, lack of materials, space, etc.) to being able to do it
- They *can't do* what they are expected to do; they don't have the ability

Once you explore which of these factors (and there could be several) are contributing to the problem, then it will be important for you to match your response. The following guidelines may help.

- If they don't know what they're supposed to do, then you need to provide them with clear expectations. That can include written guidelines or lists, demonstrations, and/or models.

- If they don't know how to do it, then you will want to provide or access the necessary training. This might include written or electronic resources, the ability to observe or shadow someone, a step-by-step guide or demonstration, or a mentor. However this is provided, feedback is essential to them becoming proficient.

- If they don't want to, you will need to explore the area of motivation. Do they not believe it is important? Do they not think it falls within their job description? Is the job that they are assigned not a good match for the individual?

- If there are roadblocks or constraints, then it will be important to see what changes need to be made in terms of schedule, reallocation of responsibilities, obtaining materials or equipment, or a location in which to work, etc.

♦ If they are not capable of doing what is expected, then it was a selection problem. If this is the situation, you will need to address it through a transfer to a position in which the person can be successful, or through the evaluation/termination process.

Chapter Summary

In order to ensure that the school operations are organized and supported to maximize student learning, you have gained a familiarity with the facility's physical plant and the people who keep it operating. Your first steps included getting to know your custodial and maintenance staff. Communicate to them their value to the building and allow them to share with you their knowledge of the building: security systems, maintenance procedures, work in progress on the building, procedures for handling rental requests, etc. Equally important is your relationship with your school secretary. Meet with your secretary early to establish communications with her/him (regular meetings, setting priorities, etc.). Your secretary is a key person in keeping procedures efficiently and effectively organized. You will want to review the myriad operational systems in place in your building: the front office, class schedules and room assignments, school calendars and the staff handbook, the budget, transportation, and food services. All of these "systems within a system" need to be reviewed and relationships nurtured to maintain their effectiveness. Finally, you have developed effective interviewing techniques to ensure that you will hire great teachers and staff members.

Hopefully, a number of ideas have occurred to you about things you could do in organizing and supporting school operations. This would be a perfect time to jot those down on your Entry Planner. Even if you find that you cannot implement all of the ideas you have, they will not be lost if you write them down. You can always come back to the ideas in coming years.

8

Accomplishment: Supporting Staff

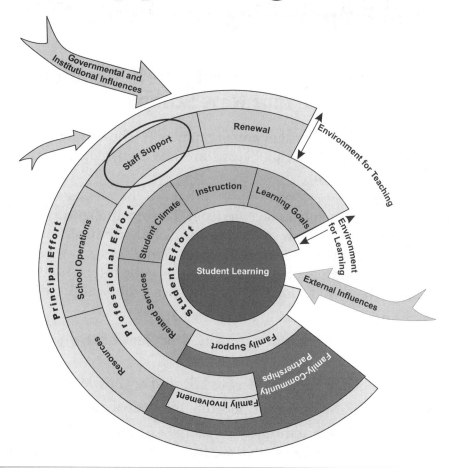

Essential Tasks
Essential Tasks
Getting Acquainted with Staff Members at Your New School
Communicating with Staff Members
Supervising and Evaluating Your Staff

8

Supporting Staff

Building Relationships Through Positive and Empowering Communication

Getting Acquainted with Staff Members at Your New School

People are the heart and soul of any organization. The accomplishment "Staff Supported" begins before the school year starts and is an integral part of each and every day of the school year.

We want to routinely ask ourselves, "What are the messages, both implicit and explicit, that staff members receive from the principal and from the school about what is expected of them, and what social and administrative support do they receive to successfully meet those expectations?" As a new principal, staff members will be observing you closely in all of your interactions and written communication. They will be looking for evidence to answer these questions:

- Is my principal interested in me and what I do?
- Does my principal take time to truly listen and hear what I have to say?
- Does my principal appreciate what I do and acknowledge my work?
- Is my principal invested in supporting me to do a good job?
- Does my principal communicate with me and the rest of the staff in a clear and timely manner so that we feel we are well informed and "in the loop"?
- Does my principal do more asking than telling?
- Is my principal committed to my success and the success of our students and school?
- Is my principal fair in making decisions and judgments involving me and the work of the school?

Recognizing your staff's scrutiny of your work and interactions, one of the most important first steps on the job is developing a personal relationship with each of your staff members. It is very natural for teachers and support staff to feel a level of anxiety about the new principal, and you can alleviate many of these fears through early, positive, and personal communication.

Communicating with Staff Members

We recommend a minimum of two forms of communication prior to the start of the school year:

1. Letter of introduction to all staff members.

2. Scheduled interviews with all staff members, with the intent of getting to know them better and giving them an opportunity to share with you their perspectives on the school and their work.

If the lateness of your appointment does not allow you to conduct individual interviews, consider one of the following:

- Group interviews, based on grade levels, departments, roles
- "Drop-in days" letting staff members know of days that you will be in the building and would welcome them to stop by and visit
- Scheduled phone conversations with staff members

In each of these communications, the four messages that you, as the new principal, want to deliver are:

1. You are a valued member of the school team

2. The work you do is very important

3. I am interested in you, as a person, and in your perspectives and opinions, to further increase our school's performance

4. I am here to support your success

Of course, the important thing about any of the communications—whether written or face-to-face oral communications—is that they convey your genuine sentiments and reflect who you are. We offer these examples as ways to express your commitment to your staff and your vision for the school and as ways to seek input from your staff. You will want to craft communications that reflect your tone, your personality, and your own leadership style.

Sample Communications

On the following pages, we have provided several examples of communications necessary for effectively interacting with your staff. All letters should be sent on school stationery.

- Letter of Introduction to the Staff (Template 13 on the following page 115)
- Introductory Interviews with Staff Members (Template 14, page 116)
- Welcome and Informational Letter to New Hires (Template 15, page 118)
- Back to School Letter to All Staff Members (Template 16, page 121)
- Staff Bulletin (Template 17, page 125)
- Personal Interactions

Template 13. Letter of Introduction to the Staff

Dear Staff of Martin Luther King Elementary School,

It is indeed my great honor to have been named, during this past week, as Principal of Martin Luther King Elementary School. Please know that I am committed to earning the trust and respect that you have shown me in providing me the opportunity to share in the leadership of your fine school.

Throughout the process of interviewing at King and learning about your school, I was repeatedly impressed with the accomplishments demonstrated by a staff committed to student success. When members of the selection committee spoke about the gains in achievement through your new literacy program and the intensive professional development you all have participated in, they spoke with well-deserved pride and a commitment to continue this growth. I commend you on these achievements. It is clear to me that you take the mission statement of your school very seriously and that it drives both the focus of your work and the manner in which you do that work each day.

"It is the mission of Martin Luther King Elementary School to provide its students with opportunities designed to meet individual needs and to ensure that every child has experiences that promote growth in each area of development. Through mutual respect within the total school community, our children will grow and learn in a positive atmosphere where faculty, staff, parents, and students together are enthusiastic about the teaching and learning process."

I commend you on the seriousness with which you take your mission at King, and I look forward to contributing to the successful realization of this mission.

I am eager to have an opportunity to meet with each of you personally and learn more about you and your work at King. I am planning to be in town all of next week, and I have asked Maria Shepherd, school secretary, to place a sign-up sheet in the staff lounge. Could I please ask that you schedule a time to meet with me that is convenient to you? Thank you, in advance, for taking this time out of your schedule.

My understanding is that you have a staff meeting scheduled on Thursday, May 7, and your principal, Samantha Miles, has graciously asked me to attend. At that time, I look forward to meeting with all of you as a staff and getting a chance to see you "in action."

Again, thank you for the opportunity to become a member of your impressive school community. It is an honor that I will work hard to deserve. I look forward to meeting with each of you next week.

Sincerely,

Template for the Letter of Introduction to the Staff can be found at www.eyeon education.com for your modification.

Template 14. Introductory Interviews With Staff Members

Introductions

Thanks so much for taking the time to come in and meet with me. How is your day going? …. The purpose for me asking to meet with each of the staff members individually is really threefold:

- I want to give you the opportunity to get to know me better and to ask any questions of me that you might have regarding this change in principals. I know having been a teacher when leadership changes have occurred, three different times, that I always felt a level of anxiety until I really had the opportunity to meet and talk with the new principal

- Second, I certainly want to get to know you better and learn how to best support your work, and

- Last, through our conversation, I hope to learn more about King Elementary, both in terms of its strengths and its challenges, from your perspective.

Possible Interview Questions

1. Can you tell me a little about yourself? Assignment and length of time working at King?

2. How would you describe what King Elementary School stands for, using four words or less?

3. What, in your opinion, is the most critical event that is happening at King that must be reinforced or protected at all costs?

4. What is the most crucial challenge that you believe we face next year, and how should we address it?

5. How are you heard at King? What opportunities or forums exist in which you can have influence?

6. In your role as _____, what is your niche or special talent/strength that allows you to positively impact students, staff, and/or community?

7. What else would you like me to know that would help to provide sound and effective leadership at King next year?

8. What questions do you have for me?

Template for Introductory Interviews with Staff can be found at www.eyeon education.com.

Welcome and Informational Letter to New Hires

You probably remember clearly getting the phone call offering you a new teaching position. You likely felt both excitement and a sense of validation that "they chose me." Then, shortly after getting the call, these emotions were followed by a long list of questions forming in your mind as well as a need to feel supported to actually "do the job." The purpose of a welcome and informational letter to all new hires is threefold:

- To sustain that excitement and enthusiasm about becoming a staff member at your school,
- To affirm the skills and talents that were communicated in the interview and let new staff members know that they are valued, and
- To provide information about support and schedules that will lower new employee anxiety.

This letter serves as one of those *important first impressions* to your new staff members. As a result of this communication, you would like the person receiving it to say, "I made the right decision in accepting this position. This is the school where I want to be, and this is the principal with whom I want to work." Consider designing your letter to include the following.

Information

- Opportunities to see the school, the classroom, and access materials for planning
- Mentor assignment and how she/he will be contacted
- How to contact you or other school personnel with questions
- Information on any special training that is either required or available for their participation

Feeling Tone

- Welcoming and enthusiastic about having them "on board"
- Endorsing what you see as their strengths and what will be their contributions to the school community
- Accessible to them and inviting of their concerns and questions
- Considerate in anticipating their needs

A sample Welcome and Informational Letter to New Hires can be found in Template 15 on the following pages.

Template 15. Welcome and Informational Letter to New Hires

Ms. Rosita Martinez
2020 Allegheny Road
Anytown, USA

Dear Rosita,

It is my pleasure to be the first to welcome you to your new school, Martin Luther King Elementary School. I so enjoyed meeting with you during the interview last week, and I am delighted that you have committed to becoming a member of our school faculty.

Several things in particular impressed both me and the other members of the committee about you during the interview process. You clearly possess a love of children and a deep commitment to their learning. Your approaches to individual goal setting and to monitoring of each students' reading and math progress that you described were exciting to hear about, and I am eager to see them in action in the classroom. The previous training and experience you bring in the area of literacy and the writing process will contribute significantly to the students' progress, as well as our overall school program. Finally, you communicated that teamwork was essential to all learners, students and teachers alike, in reaching their goals. This belief aligns well with the philosophy of our school.

I wanted to make you aware of a number of upcoming events and/or opportunities that will assist you with feeling more acclimated in your new school. If you have any questions regarding these, please feel free to give me a call (school: 333-444-5555; home: 666-777-8888).

- ◆ Each of the teachers new to our school has a mentor during their first year. Elyse Carson is the leader of your third-grade team and will also serve as your mentor. You may remember Elyse from the interview. She will be calling you soon to welcome you and to set up a time to meet with you to provide you with helpful information. At that time, she also will show you your classroom and access any teacher guides and materials you may desire for planning. Once teacher report days begin on August 9, Elyse will introduce you to staff members and take you to the district convocation. Elyse is a great person and highly knowledgeable of the school and district, so don't hesitate to ask her any questions you may have.

- ◆ I will meet with all new teachers to King on August 6, the first day for teachers new to the district to report, at 8:30 AM and we'll begin in the teacher's lounge. This will give you the opportunity to meet other new colleagues, and I will provide an orientation to the building, highlight policies and procedures from the staff handbook, address expectations, and introduce you to your "new best friends," Maria Sheherd, the school secretary, and Robert Roland, our head custodian. At that time, we also will take a drive around the King neighborhood so that you have a better feel for the community. The afternoon will be yours to work in your classroom, and Carla will provide you with any supplies you may need for this.

♦ On August 7–8, you will be engaged in district curriculum and classroom discipline training for all new staff. This is a wonderful opportunity to begin to feel comfortable with our language arts and mathematics instructional programs as well as to get a "refresher course" and some good tips on positive student behavior planning. The instructors for each of the trainings is a teacher from our district, so I believe you can count on getting relevant and practical information.

♦ A letter to all staff members will arrive in late July and will provide a schedule of activities for the days prior to children arriving.

Okay, Rosita, now that I've filled your calendar with important events, let me say "Welcome" one more time. I look forward to serving as your principal, and I know I will learn a great deal from you. Please know that I am committed to your success and to the success of your students. Best wishes for an enjoyable rest of the summer.

Sincerely,

Template for the Welcome and Information Letter to New Hires can be found at www.eyeoneducation.com for your modification.

Back to School Letter to All Staff Members

About three weeks before staff members are to report back to school, visions (and sometimes nightmares) often start creeping into teachers' previously sound summer slumbers. They begin to check their calendars and formulate questions about the coming school year, particularly if they are experiencing a change in principal leadership.

Through a strong "back to school" letter that goes to ALL staff members, you can help to provide clarity and decrease anxiety. Put yourself in the place of your staff and ask yourself what *information* and what *feeling tone* you would want conveyed to you from your new principal. Here is what some teachers have told us:

Information

♦ Who are our new staff members

♦ The basics: dates, times, agendas for all contract days prior to the students arriving

- School calendar, class schedules, enrollment information to date (e.g., "I heard that third grade was starting with 32 students in a classroom")
- Room assignments, if changes have occurred
- Status of materials that have been ordered and how to access them
- Information on any special training that either has occurred over the summer or will occur prior to school starting

Feeling Tone

- Welcoming, positive, and enthusiastic about being principal at the school
- Organized and demonstrating an attention to detail (one of most teachers' greatest fears is that structures will not be in place and fully communicated for them to do their job well)
- Accessible to staff members and inviting of their concerns and questions
- Honoring and endorsing of their talents and contributions
- Committed to supporting their success and their students success
- Considerate ("Feeding helps the meeting")
- Sense of humor

A sample Back to School Letter to All Staff Members can be found in Template 16 that follows.

Template 16. Back to School Letter to All Staff Members

Dear Staff of Martin Luther King Elementary School,

I hope this letter finds each of you enjoying the last weeks of your summer break and that you have found time to relax, spend time with family and friends, and perhaps even get in some traveling. I am very much looking forward to reconnecting with all of you whom I met last spring or over the summer, as well as meeting a few of you for the first time.

As the calendar moves from July to August, parents and children are beginning to think about setting alarm clocks, shopping for back to school supplies, and deciding on the "first day attire." As educators, August usually brings to mind a set of other thoughts: new colleagues, schedules, class lists, registration, orders received, and more. Let me use this letter to address some of these key issues and then please know that both Maria, the school secretary, and I are in the building now each day, so don't hesitate to call with more specific questions.

New Colleagues

In terms of new members of the Martin Luther King staff, I know you will join me in welcoming five new educators to our school. It has been my pleasure to work with some of you in selecting the following new members:

- Lisa Welborn, who will be taking the kindergarten position that Jane Season served in, comes to us from Oak Park, Illinois, and brings six years of teaching experience.

- Lionel Jacobs, who will be serving in the technology position, is transferring to our school from Meadow Lane, where he has been in the technology role for three years.

- Susan Thurber, who will be joining the third-grade team because of increased enrollment, has recently moved to our community from Lamar, Colorado, and she has been teaching grades 2 and 4 for seven years.

- Denise Trujillo, who will be providing both direct and support services to our special education students and filling the position previously held by Sarah Banks, is a Colorado Springs native and has been teaching in District #3 for the past three years.

- James Iida, who will be our literacy coach and is filling the position of Julie Mercer, has just moved from Greeley, where he completed a Masters in reading.

As those of you who served in the interview committees can attest, we are very fortunate to have these highly trained, experienced, and energetic teachers join our staff, and they (and I), in turn, are very lucky to have each of you "veterans" eager to show us the ropes!

Schedules

A schedule for the first days back in the building is enclosed with this letter. Specific classroom and special schedules have been completed and have been put online on the school website. If there appears to be any conflicts or errors, please let me know.

Class Lists

Class lists have been compiled to reflect all students pre-registered last spring and up through July 26, and those lists are on the school website. Additions and deletions of students will be updated as Maria gets new enrollment information. At this time, no grade levels evidence a concern regarding high or low enrollment figures, but obviously we will monitor this daily once the school year begins.

Orders Received

- All grade-level orders from the district warehouse have been received and are located in a corner of the team leader's classroom.
- Any individual teacher orders are marked with your names and are located in the art room.
- All of the new literacy program materials have been received and are located in the Literacy Coach's room.

Note: When picking up orders, please inform Maria so that she can check off all materials as being received by you. Thanks!

In Closing...

In closing, let me just say how honored I am to be serving as your principal. From the first interview last spring, I have felt and recognized the energy, talent, commitment, and spirit that exists here at Martin Luther King Elementary School. It is my desire to ensure that this school year begins with you having all the support necessary to bring success to you and your students. If there are questions or needs that I have not addressed, please do not hesitate to call or come see me.

Please enjoy these last days of summer, and I look forward to seeing you on August 9, if not before.

Best wishes,

Schedule for First Days Returning to School (August 9–12)

Monday, August 9

7:30–8:30	"Welcome and Welcome Back" Breakfast in the library
8:30–10:30	First Staff Meeting of the Year—YEAH! "Leading, Learning, Laughing, and Logistics"
10:30–12:30	Time to spend in building as needed
12:30–2:30	Grade-Level and Interdisciplinary Team Meetings
2:30–4:00*	Time to spend in building as needed

*Mitch, the night custodian, will be working his regular hours, so the building will be open until 9:30 PM if you need to stay late.

Tuesday, August 10

7:00–8:30	Continental Breakfast will be set up in the lounge "Help yourself and ease into the day"
8:30–10:00	Principal Meeting with Team Leaders
10: 00–11:00	K–1 Meeting with Literacy Coach 2–3 Meeting with Math Coach 4–5 Meeting with Counselor
12:00–1:00	K–1 Meeting with Math Coach 2–3 Meeting with Counselor 4–5 Meeting with Literacy Coach
1:30–2:30	K–1 Meeting with Counselor 2–3 Meeting with Literacy Coach 4–5 Meeting with Math Coach

All times not committed in meetings, please spend time as needed

Wednesday, August 11

7:30–8:30	District Breakfast at Sheridan High School (car pool if possible)
8:30–10:00	District "Welcome Back" Assembly (program is posted on the district website)
10:00–1:30	Return to school; spend time as needed
3:00–3:30	Brief Staff Meeting for "Final Check"; everything set to welcome students and parents tomorrow

Thursday, August 12—"It's *Show Time*: Let the Games Begin"

7:00	Pre-Game Coffee and Snacks will be in the lounge
7:45	All staff members on the grounds to welcome and guide students and parents
8:15	Bell for School to Begin/Specials Schedules begin at 9:30
9:30	Principal Classroom Visits throughout the day (specific times given at grade-level meetings)
3:00–3:15	All staff on playground to ensure students find siblings, parents, buses, etc.
3:15–4:30	Principal will check in with teams/departments to determine needs/ debrief the first day

Template for the Back to School Letter to All Staff Members can be found at www.eyeon education.com for your modification.

Staff Bulletins

Staff bulletins serve the important purpose of keeping the staff informed on upcoming events, dates and times, due dates and timelines, as well as updated information regarding building or district policy or procedure changes. Additionally, this form of communication is a great place to thank staff members and praise the work that they have done. You may be aware of the research conducted on employee motivation [results of research conducted by Glenn Tobe & Associates, cited in *The Heart of Coaching* (2000) by Thomas G. Crane]. In surveying employees about what motivated them to do their best, the following were the top three factors identified:

♦ Appreciation (public/private praise)

♦ Feeling "in the know" (informed as to what is going on in our work setting)

♦ Understanding attitude (personal concern for me)

Designing a timely, informative, and reinforcing staff bulletin that your faculty receives every week can be a significant contributor to staff morale. Bulletins typically follow an established format, with dates and events easily found at the top, followed by numbered pieces of information and feedback that are easy to track. Bulletins are generally sent out at the end of the week so that staff members can use this information to plan for the coming week. A sample weekly bulletin is included in Template 17 that follows.

Some principals provide hard copies on brightly colored, three-hole punched paper for ease in recognition and storage for reference; other principals distribute the weekly bulletin by e-mail. The key is deciding which strategy will best provide your staff with regular updates throughout the school year.

Template 17. Staff Bulletin

Weekly Update
XYZ High School
Week of August 22, 2006

Upcoming Events

Monday, Sept 2	**No School**—Labor Day. Building closed.	
Tuesday, Sept 3	**Academic Council** (Dept Chairs)	6:30 AM, Room 5
	Action Team Leaders Meeting	7:00 AM, Room 131
Wednesday, Sept 4	**Open House**	6:30–9:00 PM
Thursday, Sept 5	**Staff Work Groups** (Teachers only)	

These meetings will be held in the DWE Computer Lab on the first floor of the library during the period that you are assigned to Staff Work Groups. You will be generating up-to-date reports on your classes that include CSAP results. Learning how to do this will allow you to access information anytime that you need it.

Monday, Sept 9	Staff Meeting Time	6:30–7:30 AM

- This month, we will use the time for Action Teams to meet. If you are on an Action Team, you will be meeting from 6:30–7:30 AM in the place designated by your Action Team Leaders.

- There will also be a meeting of ninth-grade teachers with the Ninth-Grade Support Team in the Lecture Hall. If you are a teacher of freshmen and are also a member of an Action Team, please let Tom know. He will provide the information and references you need and may arrange to talk with you about it at another time.

I want to thank you for helping start this year well. I know that it was stressful for all of us. So many meetings—so much new information. I have mentioned to several that this was a difficult start for me. Having been a high school principal for so many years, you would think that it would be second nature. I suppose it would be if you, the parents, the district, and the students had the same expectations of me as you did 10 or 15 years ago. However, the times are very different now for all of us. It means that we are no longer concerned just with the "way we have always done things." Expectations have changed for all of us. It means that we each have to constantly learn new things, incorporate new skills and approaches to instruction, and count on each other to provide the support/ information we need as we move forward. It is hard! I do know that we can do it. I just think that it is important that we acknowledge that we are learning a great deal everyday and that it is not easy—it takes hard work. Once I came to that realization, it helped. I thank each of you for your constant diligence in providing only the best in instruction for our students. They deserve that!

Please read the Update carefully. There are a few changes for this week. There are also two additional attachments to the e-mail. One is a poster for your room to remind students of picture retakes. The other attachment is the revised evaluation list for the year. Once we received the corrections, it was necessary to balance responsibilities. Have a good week!

                                                                    Valerie

Updates and Information

1. No Fire Drill on Wednesday! Thanks to Matt who smelled the smoke and saw the flames from the fire in the dumpster and pulled the alarm. Always act on the side of safety. It is far better than assuming that the situation is under control. So—we had our August drill—all done!

2. Superintendent's Sounding Board: We need two teachers to represent our school. Steve and Thaddeus represented us last year. This year, Steve is not in a classroom assignment role and Thaddeus is an Action Team Leader, so we need new representatives. The Superintendent has changed the monthly meetings. Secondary reps have their own meeting with him in November and March. Elementary teachers meet with him in October and February. All reps meet in September, January, and April. It is important that the Superintendent hears you. It would be wonderful if we had one teacher who has been on staff and one new teacher. Please let me know this week if you would like to represent your peers.

3. Activity Sponsor Stipend: Please review the memo in your Start-up Packet. *If you are a club/activity sponsor, by* September 15*, you must:*

    *   Have an application on file in my office. If you have one on file from last year, you must review it, make any necessary changes, and initial/date it. *If you don't, you cannot be considered for a stipend this year.*

    *   The Stipend Committee will meet after September 15 to review all applications and to develop recommendations for the teaching staff's review, adjustment suggestions, and approval.

4. First Aid/CPR classes: These classes fill up quickly! If you want to take one, please sign up *this week* on the flier on the bulletin board across from the mailboxes. Kathy will turn in the list on Friday.

5. Facility needs: Please e-mail Angelo with any requests. Copy the e-mail to Karen. This is the only way we can keep up with requests and not let any slip through the cracks. Thanks!

6. Hallways: Thanks to those of you who have conscientiously been out in the hallways to help encourage our students to get to class on time. We do need everyone's help, please. It made a huge difference in the fourth quarter of last year. If we consistently emphasize this now, it will help all year.

7. Community Resource Bank: See Kathy for the appropriate form to request community speakers who are registered with the district.

8. Department Chairs: Our School Improvement Plan is due on September 15. Remember that your activities are due to Kathy no later than September 6. We have to compile the plans for presentation and endorsement by our Building Accountability Advisory Committee (BAAC) on September 11.

9. The Icebreaker Dance: This event, held last Friday, was a huge success! We had hundreds of students here! Congratulate the Student Council, Cabinet, Sharon, and the other sponsors for putting together a successful first event for our school!

10. Open House on Wednesday, September 4: Parents will expect to hear some pretty specific information from you that night:

   - What can I expect my student to learn?
   - How will I know the degree to which she/he is learning it?
   - What happens if she/he is not learning what she/he needs to know and do?
   - How will I be able to communicate with each teacher who works with my student?

   Remember that you will have only 15 minutes to communicate a great deal of information. It helps to have a handout with all of the information for the parents' reference. Parents make judgments about us in that brief period of time. At the conclusion of the evening, you can leave knowing that the impression you made was professional, knowledgeable, and responsive. More than anything else, parents need to know you care! Please talk to your Department Chairs if you need help preparing for this most important evening. They are most willing to model, provide feedback, and even coach you in a rehearsal; don't hesitate to call on them for the support that you need.

Key Events This Week

♦ Wednesday, August 28: All teachers on formal evaluation (reference the attachment included with this e-mail) must attend one of three sessions (30 minutes) to introduce the evaluation process and procedures. You can attend at one of the following times:

- Period 4 or 5 lunches—bring your lunch. We will meet in the Lecture Hall
- 3:20 PM in the Lecture Hall

See you there!

Have a wonderful week!

Template of the Weekly Bulletin can be found at www.eyeoneducation. com for your modifications.

Personal Interactions

It is helpful in your communication with staff to make a sweep through the building prior to classes starting in the morning and to do so as often as you can. This gives you an opportunity to greet people and wish them a good day; it also makes you accessible if someone needs to speak briefly with you. Again, this is another opportunity to validate to the staff their importance to you.

You will need to decide upon your policy for having staff stop by your office to speak with you and to communicate that policy to them. Many principals have an open door policy, and as long as they are not involved in a meeting, conversation with another person, or phone call, they encourage staff members to stop by as necessary. There will be times when it is important that you are not interrupted; at those times, the door to your office should be closed, and your secretary can schedule an appointment time or deliver a message.

You will want to survey your office to see that it is a welcoming place to staff and other visitors. An office that is cluttered or does not have several comfortable chairs for you to conduct a conversation basically gives the message, "I don't have time for you. I am not anxious to meet with you." Often times, teachers have some written information to share with you, and having a small conference table in your office where you can sit together and go over the information communicates that you wish to work together. Finally, unless someone is just stopping by and giving you a message, you will always want to come from behind your desk to visit with them. Keeping the desk between you creates distance and emphasizes your authority.

Professional Development

You will want to find out the norms that presently exist for professional development in your school.

- ♦ Are early release days or non–student days scheduled on the calendar for teachers' professional development?

- ♦ Has the content for these times already been determined for this school year based on school or district priorities?

- ♦ Is a professional development coordinator or committee available in your building that is responsible for the coordination of these events?

- ♦ What has been the procedure for teachers requesting to attend a conference?

- ♦ Are these costs budgeted to a general professional development account governed by you, or do departments, grade levels, or teams have their own budget?

- ♦ Does the district provide your school with a certain number of substitute days to cover professional development activities?

- ♦ Does the district have a cap on professional development expenses, or is the amount allocated from your building budget within your control?

- ♦ What professional development commitments have already been established by the district?

- ♦ What professional development formats are ongoing in your school (e.g., grade-level/team/department sharing of instructional strategies/common assessment development and scoring, critical friends groups, curriculum committees, action research groups, peer coaching, etc.)

- ♦ Is a practice in place for either awarding credit or monetary compensation for participation in professional development activities?

These questions can serve as a start in becoming informed as to what presently exists in your school. You will want to identify the key personnel who can provide you with this information before you begin introducing your own ideas for staff development. The adage of "honoring the old before adding the new" is a good practice to follow in this area. Additionally, you will want to take the time to determine the *needs* of your staff prior to recommending solutions and training. Many a new principal has made the mistake of requiring a specific training for her/his teachers, bringing it from her/his prior experience, whether or not it was needed (or was perceived to be needed). It will serve you and your staff well to take the necessary time to determine what professional development best supports the priorities of your school and to ensure that staff members have input into the needs, content, design, schedule, and compensation.

Beginning to Assess Your School Culture

In a landmark article entitled "Good Seeds Grow in Strong Cultures," Saphier and King (1985) contend that the foundation for school improvement is the culture of the school. If certain norms of school culture are strong, improvements in instruction will be significant, continuous, and widespread; if these norms are weak, improvements will be at best infrequent, random, and slow (p. 67). The authors go on to identify 12 cultural norms that, if strongly present in a school, will contribute significantly to teacher growth and, ultimately, student growth. We introduce these norms to you at this time to provide you with a lens to view and observe your school's culture. By culture, we use the simple definition of "how we do things around here." It is our suggestion that as you interact and observe your staff, you begin to take notice of which norms appear highly visible, consistent, and apparent, and which of the norms may not be so routinely present. Later on, during the second semester, you may want to consider using the staff survey (pages 131, 132) designed by Richard Sagor (1996) to gain your faculty's perception of the culture.

The Culture Norms That Affect School Improvement: As a New Principal, What Do I Observe in Our School?

- *Collegiality* (professional collaboration on educational issues)
- *Experimentation* (interest in exploring new, not yet proven techniques)
- *High Expectations* (pervasive push for high performance from students and teachers)
- *Trust and Confidence* (pervasive feeling that people will do what's right)
- *Tangible Support* (financial and material assistance that supports teaching and learning)
- *Reaching Out to the Knowledge Base* (using research, reading professional journals, attending workshops, etc.)
- *Appreciation and Recognition* (acknowledgment of quality student/faculty work and effort)
- *Caring, Celebration, and Humor*
- *Involvement in Decision Making*
- *Protection of What's Important* (school goals and priorities)
- *Honest, Open Communication*

School Culture Survey

Schools differ in many ways. One difference is the character of their *organizational* culture. The culture of an organization can be seen through the shared norms, values, and behavior of members of the community. This survey asks you to think about *your school* as a workplace and to assess the degree to which you see each of the following norms/values are consistent features of the work life of *the school*. It is important that you score the school on each norm.

The norms/values used in this survey were derived from the work of Matthew King and Jonathan Saphier (1985). ***Thank you for completing this survey.***

Please rate each of these norms/values on the following scale:

        1 = Almost always characteristic of our school
        2 = Generally characteristic of our school
        3 = Seldom characteristic of school
        4 = Not characteristic of our school

Remember: The focus of the survey is your school *as a whole*.

For each norm/value that you score 1 or 2, please provide a recent illustrative example of when that norm was demonstrated through individual or organizational behavior.

Norm/Value	Rating	Recent Illustrative Example(s)
1. **Collegiality** Professional collaboration on educational issues		
2. **Experimentation** Interest in exploring new, not yet proven techniques		
3. **High expectations** A pervasive push for high performance from students and teachers		
4. **Trust and confidence** Pervasive feeling that people will do what's right		
5. **Tangible support** Financial and material assistance that supports teaching/learning		

Norm/Value	Rating	Recent Illustrative Example(s)
6. **Reaching out to the knowledge base** Using research, reading professional journals, attending workshops, etc.		
7. **Appreciation and recognition** Acknowledgment of quality student/faculty work and effort		
8. **Caring, celebration, and humor**		
9. **Appreciation of leadership** Specifically, leadership provided by teachers, principals, and other professional staff		
10. **Clarity of goals**		
11. **Protection of what's important** School goals and priorities		
12. **Involvement of stakeholders in decision making** Those who will be affected by decisions are involved in making them		
13. **Traditions** Rituals and events that celebrate and support core school values		
14. **Honest, open communication**		

Excerpt from *Local Control and Accountability: How to Get It, Keep It, and Improve School Performance* (Figure 6.1), by R. Sagor, 1996, Thousand Oaks, CA: Corwin Press. Reprinted with permission.

Supervising and Evaluating Your Staff

**Our greatest contribution is to be sure
there is a teacher in every classroom who cares
that every student, every day, learns and grows
and feels like a real human being.**

Dr. Donald O. Clifton, 1924–2003

As a principal, the greatest impact you can have on the learning and well-being of the students in your school is through the selection, growth and support, supervision, and evaluation of your staff. The effect of the teacher on student achievement is unequivocally supported by the research and summarized in the following statements:

♦ Teacher expertise is the single most important determinant of student achievement. Recent studies consistently show that each dollar spent on recruiting high-quality teachers, and deepening their knowledge and skills, nets greater gains in student learning than any other use of an education dollar [Ferguson, Greenwald, Hedges, & Laine as cited in Quality Teaching: The critical key to learning (1997) by Darling-Hammond].

♦ What we have consistently found in the research, starting back in the early 1980's, is that the single largest factor affecting academic growth among students is the teacher. The teacher effects make all other effects pale in comparison (Sanders, 1998).

Given the significant impact of the teacher on student learning, the principal needs to invest considerable time, attention, and resources to ensuring the strongest and most consistent teaching performance throughout the school. In planning and preparing for this, the following areas should be addressed.

District Policies and Procedures

A starting point is to familiarize yourself with the supervision and evaluation policies and procedures outlined by the school district. You will want to review the following documents:

♦ *Job descriptions for each of the members of your staff.* Everyone needs to be clear regarding expectations.

♦ *Goals and priorities of the district and the school.* Documents such as district and school accountability and improvement plans will inform you as to areas of curricular and instructional emphasis and where feedback and support will be important.

♦ *Specific supervision and evaluation guidelines.* The district likely will have specific guidelines regarding who is scheduled for formal evaluation, the frequency of classroom observations, timelines for conferences and written reports, and the particular forms that are used. Acquaint yourself with these materials and put key dates on your calendar.

♦ *Past evaluations.* Review evaluation reports completed on staff members from the previous year. Although you may not want to use these as models and you certainly will want to gather your own data regarding individual teacher performance, this information will provide you with insight in terms of what has been done in the past as well as letting you know if any staff members are on remediation plans that need to be monitored closely.

♦ *Performance goals.* Most school districts use individual performance goals to focus the formal evaluation process. Given the school and district goals, are there specific areas you will require these performance goals to reflect? Are there a certain number of performance goals required by the district? Again, reviewing past evaluations, have goals been written in such a manner as to be clear, measurable, challenging, and lead to impacting important student learning?

Formal and Informal Supervision and Evaluation

Although formal supervision and evaluation are very important, they typically reflect the "legal and minimum" requirements of supervision. District guidelines most often answer the questions, "What is required? What is the minimum number of visits? What are the basic areas for which the supervisor needs to provide feedback?"

Clearly, to impact teacher effectiveness, you will want to extend your supervision and evaluation activities far beyond the district "minimum standards." Develop a routine from the very beginning of the school year of trying to stop by each classroom briefly each day, rotating at different times of the day. You will learn a great deal about classroom routines, time on task, teacher–student interactions, and classroom organization; this also will provide an opportunity for the teacher to connect with you if necessary. If you develop a daily schedule that allows for this "MBWA" (management by walking around) before the school year begins and teachers know to expect this, you most likely will be able to establish and maintain this valuable use of your time.

Ideally, although most of the classroom visits will be just a couple of minutes, serving to get a daily pulse of the school, shoot for targeting two classes per day when you can spend at least ten minutes to observe actual instruction. Carry with you a supply of note cards and, during the last couple of minutes in the classroom, write a brief note highlighting the positive things you observed. This "mini-feedback" will go a long way toward reinforcing the effective practices of teachers as well as providing much needed and much desired reinforcement for their hard work and talents. If you observe a practice that causes you a question or concern, design a time to meet with that teacher.

In your walk-arounds, be sure to stop in beginning teachers' classrooms each day for the first several weeks. This is important to ensure that they are given the support and assurance they need in order to be successful and to identify any issues that need to be addressed from the beginning rather than leading to problems resulting from a pattern of bad practices.

Learn from a Master

In the following pages, we provide additional information and support materials for designing and carrying out your supervision and evaluation meetings, conferences, observations, and record keeping. However, before the school year begins is a great time to find out which principals in the district are considered "master supervisors." These individuals exist in almost every district, and they have developed schedules, forms, goal-setting models, observation techniques, etc., that they most likely would be more than happy to share with you. Ask your supervisor to identify those "master supervisors" for you and ask one of them if, early on in the year, they can share their strategies and possibly even have you sit in on the initial evaluation meeting with staff as well as a classroom observation and feedback conference.

Evaluation of Licensed Personnel

Your school district will have specific policies and procedures regarding the formal evaluation of your professional teaching staff. These policies will outline who is to be evaluated in terms of the probationary teachers, the cycle of experienced teachers who typically have completed three continuous years, and any teachers who may be on a plan of remediation. It will be important for you to review this list of staff members early in the school year.

Additionally, the policies and procedures will most often include district performance standards, the minimum number of classroom observations and conferences required, formats for goal setting and conferences, use of data sources, and timelines for the completion of the various evaluation components. It is also common for a district to require the principal to hold an evaluation orientation meeting for all faculty members involved in the evaluation process within the first 30 days of the school year.

On the next page, you will find an example (Template 18 on page 136) that you can revise as needed to record the staff members under evaluation, all of the required stages of the evaluation process and their due dates, and when you have scheduled these events with each staff member. It will be important to mark these dates in your personal calendar, along with reminder dates to schedule the next set of observations and conferences.

Template 18. Teacher Evaluation Activities Chart

Activities/Due Dates

Teachers in Evaluation Cycle and Status*	Staff Evaluation Orientation 9/30	Job Targets Set and Conf Conducted 10/15	Pre-Observation Conf #1	Observation #1 11/30	Post-Observation Conf #1 12/15	Pre-Observation Conf #2	Observation #2 2/15	Post-Observation Conf #2 3/1	Mid-year Written Eval (Optional)	Final Appraisal Conf 5/15	Written Eval Form Signed 5/30
1. Akers, Jan (P)											
2. Bonds, Brian (E)											
3. Parker, Pat (R)											
4.											
5.											
6.											
7.											
8.											
9.											

*E = experienced; P = probationary; R = remediation plan

Template of the Teacher Evaluation Activities Chart can be found at www.eyeoneducation.com for your modification.

A Reflection Exercise for Designing the Evaluation Experience for Your Staff Members

Likely, you have had a number of experiences in the evaluation process when you served as a teacher being evaluated. In talking with numerous educators about their evaluation experiences, they tell many stories, both good and bad, about these experiences. We suggest that by reflecting on your experiences as an *evaluatee*, you can gain clarity about what behaviors and structures you want to put in place to ensure a positive and growth-promoting experience for those staff members who you are now getting ready to evaluate.

Take time, sit back, and think about your past experiences in being evaluated by your principal(s) or supervisor(s). What were your BEST experiences? What were your WORST experiences? What were the specifics of the situations? How did you feel about these experiences?

From these recollections, make two lists for yourself. The first list is entitled "My Ideal List." Under this heading, list the generalizations that you draw from your best experiences. Some things that possibly come to mind are "I clearly understood the process and what the expectations were for my performance"; "My evaluator provided me with specific feedback that really helped me improve my teaching"; and "My evaluator was really committed to my growth and provided me both encouragement and the resources to get better."

The second list is entitled "My Never-Ever List." Under this heading, list the generalizations that are drawn from your worst experiences. These are things that you never ever want to find yourself doing in the role as evaluator. Some things that other principals have listed are "My evaluator never came in to observe me and yet made judgments about my performance"; "When we conferenced following the observation, my principal spent most of the time talking and was not interested in my thinking or my reflections on the lesson"; and "I felt like this was something that my principal just needed to get done and was not interested in me or using this as an opportunity to help me grow professionally."

By taking the time to reflect on your past experiences with evaluation, you can enter your new role as a supervisor by building on these experiences and using them as guidance in utilizing best practices.

Preparing for Your First Staff Orientation to the Evaluation Process

Whether or not your district *requires* an orientation to the evaluation process for those staff members who are being evaluated, it is a very helpful and efficient practice. At this time, you can provide your staff with a clear understanding of the process, some tools for self-assessing their professional skills and writing important goals, and the timelines to be adhered to throughout the school year. It is also a time to demonstrate your commitment to their professional learning and growth.

A possible outline for the agenda of this evaluation orientation might be:

♦ Thank the staff members for coming and let them know that you are looking forward to working with them in the evaluation process. Communicate to them that you enter into this process in the spirit of mutual learning and growth.

♦ Provide copies of the district process for evaluation and highlight the key steps and timelines.

♦ Provide copies of their respective job descriptions and the district professional performance standards. These two documents outline the criteria with which licensed personnel are evaluated.

♦ Consider providing copies of the "Standards for Effective Teaching Framework" (Danielson, 1996) for teachers to conduct a self-evaluation of their teaching skills and practice. An outline of the domains and components included in the framework as well as a sample rubric begin on page 141 in this chapter. The complete framework can be found in *Enhancing Professional Practice: A Framework for Teaching* (Danielson, 1996). Teachers who have used this framework as a self-assessment and in preparation of identifying professional goals have indicated that the process was one of the most insightful activities that they have engaged in as an educator.

♦ In many districts, staff members under evaluation are asked to develop, with guidance from their principal, one to three measurable goals that reflect the professional performance standards (i.e., effective instruction, management of learning environment, interpersonal skills, professional characteristics) and that would contribute to the staff members' professional growth and, ultimately, to student achievement. If your district requires the development of these goals, it is helpful to provide resources and models for writing these goals. This support typically contributes greatly to the writing of goals that are both meaningful and measurable. We have provided examples of possible support materials for writing goals (Template 19, page 139).

♦ Provide opportunities for staff members to ask questions regarding the process.

♦ Have a calendar available for staff members to sign up for their initial conference with you where the two of you will review and finalize the professional goals and schedule the first classroom observation.

Template 19. Assisting Teachers in Writing Professional Goals

A Process for Writing Strong Professional Goals

Determine the Focus

Your professional goals should be grounded in content and skill areas that, if met, will have a significant impact on your teaching performance and, ultimately, on your students' achievement. Many teachers say that the hardest part of the evaluation process is coming up with *meaningful goals*; meaningful goals are those that will have a positive impact on your teaching performance, that you are interested in investing your time and energy, and that will benefit from focused attention. To support you in identifying meaningful goals for your evaluation year, here are some suggestions.

1. Take time to review the district performance standards that outline the expectations for the district's professional staff. Highlight any areas in which you may have an interest in further developing your expertise.

2. Next, using the "Standards for Effective Teaching Framework" (Danielson, 1996) and a highlighter pen, conduct a self-evaluation of your teaching skills, as you perceive that you routinely demonstrate them at this point in your teaching career. For most of us, there will be areas that are highly developed and possibly at the distinguished level, whereas others fall in the basic or proficient areas. Once you have completed your self-evaluation, review it to identify possible areas for the development of *meaningful goals*. Please know that the "Standards for Effective Teaching Framework" is given to you for your own self-evaluation purposes only. You will not be asked to provide a copy of your self-evaluation to the principal, and it is your choice as to whether to share parts or none of the instrument when discussing your goals.

3. Finally, you may choose to do some professional reading that will help to generate areas of focus for your goals and also possibly discuss developing common goals with colleagues who are also being evaluated.

4. The following questions may assist you in finalizing your meaningful goals:

   • What student content standard(s) is significant in my course/grade level and requires particular attention to increase student achievement? In reviewing past student achievement data, are there important content or skill areas that students have particular difficulty mastering?

   • Are there specific district/school/team/grade-level/department goals that I am encouraged to align my professional goals with?

   • Based on my self-evaluation on the "Standards for Effective Teaching Framework," are there areas I've identified that, if I further developed or refined, would make me a more effective teacher?

- Are there particular models of teaching, or strategies, that I want to investigate and test their effectiveness with my students?
- Are there new professional roles to which I aspire and for which I wish to further develop competencies?

Write the Goal(s)

Effective goals:

♦ Focus on an important result that reflects one or more of the district professional standards

♦ Are measurable, tangible, and verifiable

♦ Are realistic and attainable

♦ Are challenging; the goal should represent an improvement over the past

♦ Have a time limit

♦ Are put in writing

Review the Goal(s)

♦ Will my goal, if met, have a significant impact on my teaching performance and, ultimately, on my students' achievement?

♦ Will the plan of action likely result in improving student learning? Will it stretch my present skill level as a teacher?

♦ Do the assessment criteria clearly indicate to what degree the goal was met? Are there direct data that can be gathered and aggregated?

Template of Writing Professional Goals can be found at www.eyeoneducation. com for your modification.

Standards for Effective Teaching Framework

Domain 1: Planning and Preparation

Component 1a: Demonstrating Knowledge of Content and Pedagogy

- Knowledge of content
- Knowledge of prerequisite relationships
- Knowledge of content-related pedagogy

Component 1b: Demonstrating Knowledge of Students

- Knowledge of characteristics of age-group
- Knowledge of students' varied approaches to learning
- Knowledge of students' skills and knowledge
- Knowledge of students' interests and cultural heritage

Component 1c: Selecting Instructional Goals

- Value
- Clarity
- Suitability for diverse students
- Balance

Component 1d: Demonstrating Knowledge of Resources

- Resources for teaching
- Resources for students

Component 1e: Designing Coherent Instruction

- Learning activities
- Instructional materials and resources
- Instructional groups
- Lesson and unit structure

Component 1f: Assessing Student Learning

- Congruence with instructional goals
- Criteria and standards
- Use for planning

Domain 2: The Classroom Environment

Component 2a: Creating an Environment of Respect and Rapport

- Teacher interaction with students
- Student interaction

Component 2b: Establishing a Culture for Learning

- Teacher interaction with students
- Student interaction

Component 2c: Managing Classroom Procedures

- Management of instructional groups
- Management of transitions
- Management of materials and supplies
- Performance of non-instructional duties
- Supervision of volunteers and paraprofessionals

Component 2d: Managing Student Behavior

- Expectations
- Monitoring of student behavior
- Response to student misbehavior

Component 2e: Organizing Physical Space

- Safety and arrangement of furniture
- Accessibility to learning and use of physical resources

Domain 3: Instruction

Component 3a: Communicating Clearly and Accurately

- Directions and procedures
- Oral and written language

Component 3b: Using Questioning and Discussion Techniques

- Quality of questions
- Discussion techniques
- Student participation

Component 3c: Engaging Students in Learning

- Representation of content
- Activities and assignments
- Grouping of students
- Instructional materials and resources
- Structure and pacing

Component 3d: Providing Feedback to Students

- Quality, accurate, substantive, constructive, and specific
- Timeliness

Component 3e: Demonstrating Flexibility and Responsiveness

- ♦ Lesson adjustment
- ♦ Response to students
- ♦ Persistence

Domain 4: Professional Responsibilities

Component 4a: Reflecting on Teaching

- ♦ Accuracy
- ♦ Use in future teaching

Component 4b: Maintaining Accurate Records

- ♦ Student completion of assignments
- ♦ Student progress in learning
- ♦ Non-instructional records

Component 4c: Communicating With Families

- ♦ Information about the instructional program
- ♦ Information about individual students
- ♦ Engagement of families in the instructional program

Component 4d: Contributing to the School and District

- ♦ Relationships with colleagues
- ♦ Service to the school
- ♦ Participation in the school and district projects

Component 4e: Growing and Developing Professionally

- ♦ Enhancement of content knowledge and pedagogical skill
- ♦ Service to the profession

Component 4f: Showing Professionalism

- ♦ Service to the students
- ♦ Advocacy
- ♦ Decision making

Excerpt from *Enhancing Professional Practice: A Framework for Teaching,* by C. Danielson, 1996, Alexandria, VA: Association for Supervision and Curriculum Development. Reprinted with permission.

Domain 2: The Classroom Environment

Component 2c: Managing Classroom Procedures

Management of instructional groups

Management of transitions

Supervision of volunteers and paraprofessionals

Management of materials and supplies

Performance of non-instructional duties

Level of Performance

Element	Unsatisfactory	Basic	Proficient	Distinguished
Management of Instructional Groups	Students not working with the teacher are not productively engaged in learning.	Tasks for group work are partially organized resulting in some off-task behavior when teacher is involved with one group.	Tasks for group work are organized and groups are managed so that most students are engaged at all times.	Groups working independently are productively engaged at all times with students assuming responsibility for productivity.
Management of Transitions	Much time is lost during transitions.	Transitions are sporadically efficient resulting in some loss of instructional time.	Transitions occur smoothly, with little loss of instructional time.	Transitions are seamless, with students assuming some responsibility for efficient operation.
Management of Materials and Supplies	Materials are handled inefficiently, resulting in loss of instructional time.	Routines for handling materials and supplies function moderately well.	Routines for handling materials and supplies occur smoothly with little loss of instructional time.	Routines for handling materials and supplies are seamless with students assuming some responsibility for efficient operation.
Performance of Non-Instructional Duties	Considerable instructional time is lost in performing non-instructional duties.	Systems for performing non-instructional duties are fairly efficient resulting in little loss of instructional time.	Efficient systems for performing non-instructional duties are in place resulting in minimal loss of instructional time.	Systems for performing non-instructional duties are well established, with students assuming considerable responsibility for efficient operation.
Supervision of Volunteers and Paraprofessionals	Volunteers and paraprofessionals have no clearly defined duties or do nothing most of the time.	Volunteers and paraprofessionals are productively engaged during portions of class time but require frequent supervision.	Volunteers and paraprofessionals are productively and independently engaged during the entire class.	Volunteers and paraprofessionals make a substantive contribution to the classroom environment.

Excerpt from *Enhancing Professional Practice: A Framework for Teaching*, by C. Danielson, 1996, Alexandria, VA: Association for Supervision and Curriculum Development. Reprinted with permission.

Chapter Summary

In order to ensure that your staff is supported, you must take specific actions to build positive and professional relationships with each member. You have reflected on your interactions and communications with your staff members, knowing that they, too, are watching and reviewing your interactions with them and their colleagues. You have initiated positive communications with staff members in a variety of ways: a letter of introduction, staff interviews, phone conferences, letters to new hires, and back to school letters to your faculty. As the year starts up and progresses, you have provided staff bulletins and have daily personal interactions with your staff. In addition, you have reviewed job descriptions of the various positions in your building so that you know your faculty's professional roles and duties. You have developed a routine to supervise and evaluate your faculty in ways that are fair and informative and that promote the professional development of each member of your staff. You will want to ensure that staff members see the evaluation process as an important part of their professional growth and as vital to the student achievement goals of your building. Given the numerous ways you wish to support your staff, return to your Entry Planner, listing the tasks and corresponding timeline.

9

Accomplishment: Supporting School Renewal

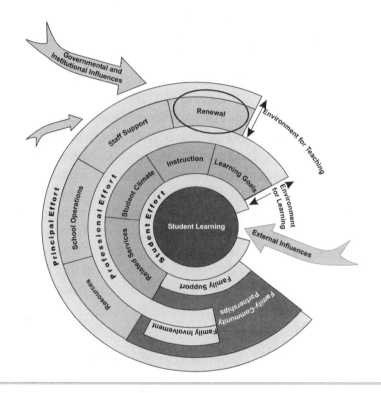

Essential Tasks

Understanding the Organizational Structure of Your School

Making Decisions in Your School

Building an Understanding of Your New School's Strengths and Needs

School Improvement Planning

Designing Your First Staff Meeting

9

Supporting School Renewal

Reviewing and Refining Processes for School Improvement

Understanding the Organizational Structure of Your School

The structures and forums in place within a school to provide venues for information giving, dialog, advisement, collaboration, study, and special purpose work are its *organization*. Forums have different purposes that must be clearly identified and understood by the school community. The clarity of the organizational design and effectiveness of the communication links between forums will either promote or detract from the school's primary work: supporting the learning of each child in the school. For example, most schools have several *advisory* forums. Parents and community members' forum for that purpose usually is the Building Accountability and Advisory Committee. The staff's forum is generally a representative group of staff who compose the Principal's Advisory Committee. Secondary schools often have student advisory groups as well. Names for the groups often reflect the purpose of the forum.

Recommendations

1. Study and understand how your school is organized.

    ♦ Are the purposes for each forum clearly defined and understood by the school community?

    ♦ As you study the organization of the school, which forums are in place to promote:

        • Information sharing?

        • Advisement?

        • Collaboration?

        • Study and dialog?

        • Special purpose work?

- Capacity building?
♦ Each of the purposes listed above is essential in a healthy school's organization. Are there gaps that you need to address?

2. If there are noticeable gaps in organizational structure or confusion about forum purposes:

♦ What *refinements* are necessary as you begin the school year?

♦ What changes need to be studied over the long term for consideration or development?

Caution: Making major, unilateral decisions about the structures and organization of the school almost always causes problems. The term "refinements" used in the bullet above is intentional.

The following tools and templates are included for your use:

♦ An example (Template 20, page 150) for analyzing organizational structures/purposes: *How are People Heard in Your School? How Do They Have Influence?*

♦ An example (Template 21, page 154) for defining group purposes/operational guidelines: *Group Charter and Session Agenda*

♦ A process tool (Template 22, page 156) for group use in norm development: *Developing Group Norms*

Template 20. How are People Heard in Your School?
How Do They Have Influence? (Example)

For each Stakeholder Group, list the forum(s) that currently exists for the purposes listed on the left.

Stakeholder Groups: Examples					
Forum Purposes	**Teachers**	**Other Staff**	**Parents**	**School Community Members**	**Students**
Information Sharing	Staff Meetings				
Advisement			Building Accountability Committee		
Collaboration				Partners Council	
Study/Dialog		Noncertified Staff Council			
Special Purpose Work					Student Government
Capacity Building	Brown-Bag Lunch Book Study				

Essential Questions:
Building Your Understanding of the Current Organizational Structure

♦ Are the purposes for each forum clearly defined and understood by members of your school community?

♦ Each of the purposes listed above is essential in a healthy school's organization. Are there gaps that you need to address? If there are noticeable gaps in organizational structure or confusion about forum purposes:

• What refinements are necessary as you begin the school year?

• What changes need to be studied over the long term for consideration or development?

Template for How Are People Heard in Your School can be found at www.eyeon education.com and on page 151.

Template 20. How are People Heard in Your School? How Do They Have Influence?

For each Stakeholder Group, list the forum(s) that currently exists for the purposes listed on the left.

Stakeholder Groups					
Forum Purposes	Teachers	Other Staff	Parents	School Community Members	Students
Information Sharing					
Advisement					
Collaboration					
Study/Dialog					
Special Purpose Work					
Capacity Building					

Essential Questions:
Building Your Understanding of the Current Organizational Structure

- ♦ Are the purposes for each forum clearly defined and understood by members of your school community?

- ♦ Each of the purposes listed above is essential in a healthy school's organization. Are there gaps that you need to address? If there are noticeable gaps in organizational structure or confusion about forum purposes:

  - What refinements are necessary as you begin the school year?

  - What changes need to be studied over the long term for consideration or development?

Group Charter and Session Agenda

Rationale

Groups are able to accomplish significant outcomes if their work is focused, the parameters are established, and time together is maximized.

Suggestions for Use

Groups, task forces, or committees can use this process and template to bring clarity to their purpose, their target and their operations.

Establishing Purpose

I. Overall Purpose:

Definition of the expected outcome(s) and the reason for a group to invest time, energy, and expertise are essential.

♦ As a group, have each member verbalize his/her understanding of the team's purpose.

♦ Write each statement on newsprint.

♦ After all statements are written, members may ask clarifying questions.

♦ Identify similarities and differences.

♦ Assure that questions are answered and misunderstandings are clarified.

♦ As a group, create a statement of the team's overall purpose that:

   • Describes the content of the project/work

   • States what the expected outcome is

   • Identifies quantifiable, measurable outcomes

   • Clearly identifies the reasons for the task/project/work

II. Non-Purpose:

Discussion and clear identification of what is *not* within the purview of a team establishes parameters for the team's work, allows the team to be aware of times when the group goes off-task and eliminate them, and brings further clarity to the overall purpose.

   • Facilitate a timed brainstorming session related to what the team is *not* about.

   • Allow participants to ask clarifying questions following the brainstorm.

- Assure questions are answered and misunderstandings are clarified.
- As a group, create a statement or concise bulleted list of non-purposes.

Examples of Purposes and Non-Purposes

Purpose:	Identify problems and criteria for solutions
Non-purpose:	Select solutions for other groups to implement
Purpose:	Ensure parental involvement in decision making
Non-purpose:	Make or approve all decisions that involve parents

---

III. Purpose of Each Session:

Clear identification of the purposes for each session brings focus to team-work and allows members to concretely identify accomplishments.

- Use this as the first and last agenda items for each session
- As each session begins, the facilitator reviews that day's purposes and verbalizes the connection between the purposes and the agenda items that follow.
- As each session ends, go back to the purposes and evaluate progress toward the purposes.
- Identify any tasks that need to be completed and assign responsibilities.
- As a group, develop a purpose and an agenda for the next session. The session purpose:
  - States what the group will do at the next session
  - Is clear and specific
  - Brings tighter focus to what is expected at the end of a session
  - Identifies what is "deliverable" at the end of the session

Template 21. Group Charter and Session Agenda (Example)

Team Name: Scheduling Committee	

Overall Purpose

- Identify problems with current daily schedule
- Identify attributes of current daily schedule
- Research best practices and make recommendations to leadership team

Non-Purpose

Selection solutions for other groups to implement.

Session Purpose

To familiarize committee with purposes, identify roles and responsibilities, develop process for work.

Date of Session: October 10   **Time:** 3:30 PM   **Location:** Media Center

Agenda

I.   Review of session purpose and agenda

II. Identification of tasks, roles, and responsibilities
- Develop committee norms and calendar of meetings

III. Process discussion

IV. Session review
- What did we accomplish
- Tasks and assignments in preparation for next session

V.   Next Session
- Purpose development
- Agenda development

Template for the Group Charter and Session Agenda can be found at www.eyeon education.com and on page 155.

Template 21. Group Charter and Session Agenda

Team Name:

Overall Purpose
•
•
•

Non-Purpose
Session Purpose
.

Date of Session:	Time:	Location:

Agenda

Template 22. Developing Group Norms (Example)

Norms are operating procedures/agreements that define behaviors. The members of the group understand and agree to behave within their group in accordance with the norms. The behaviors are described in short, clear statements and typically are based on values that are important to the group members.

Norms are important because they are formal "rules of engagement" when the group is operating. It is imperative that group members put the norms into action and feel comfortable in asking each other to adhere to them. If that does not happen, there will still be norms, but they will be unwritten, reflected by the behavior in the group, will not be understood by all, and usually undermine the group's ability to work meaningfully together. Norms are critical in establishing a climate that encourages and allows all members of the group to participate with confidence.

Group norms:

- Are few in number, easy to remember, and reviewed often by the group
- Are explicit and understandable, and describe desired acceptable behavior of group members

1. Together, identify values that are important to members of your group.

2. Select two or three of the value categories. What behaviors would put these values into action? Write statements that describe these behaviors.
    - Example:
      Value category: Open and respectful communication
      The norm: Listen well to one another without interruption

3. Be prepared to share your norm "nominations."

4. The statements will be listed for each group member to reflect on and to assign a personal level of support **prior** to coming to a group consensus.

Template for Developing Group Norms can be found at www.eyeoneducation.com and on page 157.

Template 22. Developing Group Norms

Norms are operating procedures/agreements that define behaviors. The members of the group understand and agree to behave within their group in accordance with the norms. The behaviors are described in short, clear statements and typically are based on values that are important to the group members.

Norms are important because they are formal "rules of engagement" when the group is operating. It is imperative that group members put the norms into action and feel comfortable in asking each other to adhere to them. If that does not happen, there will still be norms, but they will be unwritten, reflected by the behavior in the group, will not be understood by all, and usually undermine the group's ability to work meaningfully together. Norms are critical in establishing a climate that encourages and allows all members of the group to participate with confidence.

Group norms:
- Are few in number, easy to remember, and reviewed often by the group
- Are explicit and understandable, and describe desired acceptable behavior of group members

---

1. Together, identify values that are important to members of your group.

2. Select two or three of the value categories. What behaviors would put these values into action? Write statements that describe these behaviors.

   ■

   ■

3. Be prepared to share your norm "nominations."

4. The statements will be listed for each group member to reflect on and to assign a personal level of support **prior** to coming to a group consensus.

Making Decisions In Your School

School Governance

The term "school governance" is used in a myriad of ways. The processes in your school that result in decisions being made is *governance*. The scope of decisions that the school is permitted to make is shaped by your district's broader vision of governance. Regardless of where your district falls in the continuum of governance from site based to central control, *how* decisions are made in your school is critical. People generally do not balk at decisions if they know *how* and *why* they were made.

It is important that you take the time to discover how decisions have been made in your school and by whom. Following your analysis of that information, you will need to reconcile past practices in your new school with your personal and professional views on decision making. You will need to carefully consider what information needs to be communicated to your staff and how it can be best heard and understood.

A variety of decision-making models and successful strategies are available. The specific models or strategies that you choose to use are less important than the consistency with which they are used and the degree to which your staff and school community understand and operate with them.

This section includes guiding questions and tools for you to use in analyzing how decisions are currently made in your school, clarifying your beliefs and practices, and describing strategies that you might utilize to extend the understanding of decision making in your school and your school community.

Information and Ideas about Decision Making

How are decisions made in your school? Who makes them? If you haven't had the opportunity to ask these questions of your staff members yet, it is important that you be able to find out what staff perceptions are before you begin to tweak the system to implement your own strategies for making decisions. Why? It is important to understand where your staff members are so that you can better help them shift their thinking to where you want them to operate. If the shift is significant, they may resist the change without structured help and information.

Working with Staff: Deciding How to Decide

The following information can be modified to suit unique school needs. Principals can incorporate information from the charts, templates, handouts, and text for use with staff members. This will allow principals to develop an activity-oriented session with staff that can provide valuable information about their perceptions of the school's past practices in decision making. In addition, it will provide information for the staff and can help build common understandings among the staff that can forge a foundation for future work in the school.

Chart One, adapted from the "Levels of Influence" model of the Colorado Staff Development Council materials entitled *Facilitative Leadership* (1994), is a good way to introduce the concept of influence. It can assist you in helping staff realize that everyone in the school has influence through their actions, attitudes, and behavior.

Chart One: Levels of Influence

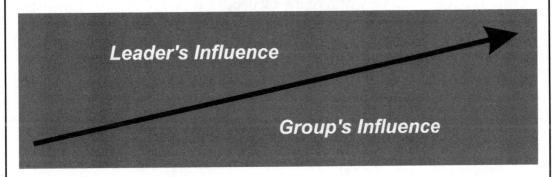

Command	Consult	Vote	Consensus
Leader or representative makes decision; involvement does not add value	Leader presents tentative decision; Invites suggestions; Discloses decision to larger stakeholder group	Leader presents several quality options; discussion; vote	Leader presents issue; all impacted solution-build until agreement is supported by all

Adapted from *Facilitative Leadership*, by the Colorado Staff Development Council, 1994, Morrison, CO: Colorado Staff Development Council.

The decisions that we make in schools involve the influence of others to varying degrees. Different issues require different strategies for decision making. No one method is appropriate for all issues. In the chart above, the bar at the top of the diagram illustrates increasing group influence on decisions as you move from left to right. The four terms at the bottom—Command, Consult, Vote, and Consensus—are common labels describing four different levels of influence. Each one is defined below.

Term	Definition
Command	The principal or representative leader makes decision and informs others; involvement does not add value to the quality of the decision.
Consult	The principal or representative leader presents a tentative decision; invites suggestions; discloses decision to larger stakeholder group.
Vote	The principal or representative leader presents several quality options; discussion; vote.
Consensus	The principal or representative leader presents issue; all who are impacted solution build until agreement is supported by all.

Although the terms *command, consult,* and *vote* are easily understood, the term *consensus* is understood very differently by people, usually based on past experiences that may or may not have been true consensus processes. For that reason, it bears discussion. Chart Two can be adapted into a visual display for use in discussion with staff.

Chart Two: Defining Consensus

Consensus Means

- All group members contribute
- Everyone's opinion is heard and encouraged
- Differences are viewed as helpful
- Everyone can paraphrase the issues
- Everyone has a chance to express thoughts about the issue
- Those who disagree indicate a willingness to experiment for a certain period of time
- All members hear the final decision
- All members agree to take responsibility for implementing the final decision

Facilitative Leadership Colorado Staff Development Council (1994)

Consensus Does *Not* Mean

- A unanimous vote
- The result is everyone's first choice
- Everyone agrees (there may only be enough support for the decision carried out)
- Conflict or resistance will be overcome immediately

Facilitative Leadership, Colorado Staff Development Council (1994)

Additionally, included for your use (page 161), is a full-page handout with a more detailed definition of consensus. It can be duplicated and given to staff for their reference during the discussion.

Consensus Handout

Consensus

Advantages to Consensus

Unlike a majority vote, consensus requires a full commitment from all the group members to the decision.

In a "vote," members in the minority often are not given an opportunity to propose changes, and if they vote NO, they are, in effect, relieved of any responsibility for the outcome. In consensus, everyone is involved at some level in the decision-making process and must indicate agreement. For this reason, the outcome is likely to be accepted by most.

Consensus may take a bit more time in a group, but the outcome is likely to be implemented and supported. It is worth the effort.

Consensus Means:

- ♦ All group members contribute
- ♦ Everyone's opinion is encouraged and heard
- ♦ Differences are viewed as helpful
- ♦ Everyone can paraphrase the issues
- ♦ Everyone has a chance to express thoughts and feelings about the issue
- ♦ Those who disagree indicate a willingness to experiment for a certain period of time
- ♦ All members hear the final decision
- ♦ All members agree to take responsibility for implementing the final decision

Consensus Does NOT Mean:

- ♦ A unanimous vote
- ♦ The result is *everyone's* first choice
- ♦ Everyone agrees (there may be only enough support for the decision to be carried out)
- ♦ Conflict or resistance will be overcome immediately

From *Facilitative Leadership*, by the Colorado Staff Development Council, 1994, Morrison, CO: Colorado Staff Development Council.

To this point, staff has been introduced to the concept of *levels of influence* and the definitions of four types of decision-making processes. The point remains to be made that the use of a specific process must be based on the issue at hand. One way to make this point is to distribute the full-page handout on page 163 titled *Decision-Making Types and Characteristics.* Decision types are listed along the left. Characteristics of the decision types are listed along the top axis. Have the staff work in small groups. Direct them to consider each decision type and to place checkmarks under the characteristics that apply.

Example:

	Quickness
Command	X

After staff report out, the point is easily made that appropriate use of decision types is situational.

Template 23. Decision-Making Types and Characteristics

	Quickness	Accuracy	Commitment	Understanding	Creativity	Readiness
Command						
Consult						
Vote						
Consensus						

Adapted from *Facilitative Leadership*, by the Colorado Staff Development Council, 1994, Morrison, CO: Colorado Staff Development Council.

Once this basic understanding is on the table, it is time to provide time and structure for the staff to explore how decisions have been made in the school. One way to do this is to distribute the full-page handout, *How Have Decisions Been Made in Our School* on page , to each staff member. Walk the staff through this handout by reviewing the definition of each decision type and then asking staff members to give an example of each decision-making method from current/past practice in the school. After you have an example for each decision-making method, have the staff work in small groups to list additional examples and to answer the three questions at the bottom on the handout. Reporting out orally will be important to allow all staff to hear examples and opinions from different groups. Collect the written answers for your use. Be sure to have your secretary make notes for your reference later. These notes and completed handouts will more clearly help you understand "how business has been done" than any other information you may collect.

Caution: Be very careful not to make judgmental statements during staff examples. If you do, voluntary comments will quickly shut down or be modified to meet what the staff members think you want to hear.

Template 24. How Have Decisions Been Made in Our School?

Methods	Definition	Examples of Our Current Practice
Command	The principal or representative leader makes decision and informs others; involvement does not add value to the quality of the decision	▪ ▪ ▪ ▪ ▪
Consult	The principal or representative leader presents a tentative decision; Invites suggestions; Discloses decision to larger stakeholder group	▪ ▪ ▪ ▪ ▪
Vote	The principal or representative leader presents several quality options; discussion; vote	▪ ▪ ▪ ▪ ▪ ▪
Consensus	The principal or representative leader presents issue; all impacted solution-build until agreement is supported by all	▪ ▪ ▪ ▪ ▪ ▪

1. How do our current decision-making practices facilitate our ability to support student learning?
2. How do they interfere?
3. Do any of our current practices need to be tweaked? How?

Please use the back of this page to record your group's responses to the questions.

Select one group member to summarize your work to the full group.

Template for How Have Decisions Been Made in Our School can be found at www.eyeoneducation.com.

Next Steps

If necessary, use what you have learned to tweak current practice. You also may identify major problems; ask a group of staff to devise suggestions for improvement of the problems. For the staff, clearly identify the next steps for improving the school's decision-making model. This is a good time to ask for staff volunteers to work on this with you. Establish a timeline for reporting back to staff. Follow through. Staff will be willing to work with you on important issues *if*:

♦ They know that you will use the information they share

♦ The process that will be used to incorporate their input is well defined

♦ The staff is given the opportunity to work with you

♦ The staff can count on the fact that there will be follow through.

Building an Understanding of Your New School's Strengths and Needs

Building a comprehensive understanding and knowledge base related to your school's trends, strengths, and needs is an expected and necessary foundation for providing insightful and effective school leadership. In your initial staff interviews, contacts with parents, students, community members, and central administrators, you will hear a variety of perspectives related to your school's needs. Having a data-based frame of reference will afford you needed perspective as you gather information and build relationships with your school community. It also will allow you to provide information to help others develop an increased understanding that will facilitate the identification of priority needs for focus and resources.

Your personal understanding and knowledge base will expand over time, however, so it is essential that you take some steps to build a foundational understanding of the school's status, trends, past initiatives, and current goals. Your ability to communicate accurately with school stakeholders and to provide information that demonstrates your understanding of the school's needs fosters a sense of "legitimacy." You care, you understand, you are equal to the task at hand, you deserve to have this position. A wealth of information is available; however, your goal right now is to establish *a basic understanding* upon which you can expand over time.

We recommend that you invest time reviewing:

♦ Achievement results and trend reports

♦ Related school data available to you

♦ Previous year's School Improvement Plan (SIP) and year-end report

♦ Draft SIP for the upcoming school year

We have included the following tools to assist you:

♦ A list of data sources (page 167)

♦ A set of questions to guide your initial data study (page 168)

Template 25. List of Data Sources for Your Initial Review: Current and Trend Data

Standardized Data Sources
- ◆ Achievement Assessment Results
- ◆ Adequate Yearly Progress (AYP)
- ◆ ACT/SAT/PSAT/PACT

District Data Sources
- ◆ District Assessments
- ◆ Demographic Data: School and District
  - Ask your supervisor for any other data that your district monitors and values

School Data
- ◆ Student Data
  - Attendance rates
  - Discipline reports
  - Graduation rates
  - Drop-out rates
  - Failure rates/retention rates
  - Permits in versus permits out
  - Individual Literacy Plan (ILP) data
  - Special Education Data
    - Number and percentage of students served
    - Programs available and staffed
  - English Language Learners (ELL) data
    - Number and percentage of students served
    - Programs available and staffed
  - Free and reduced lunch data
    - Number and percentage of students served
    - Programs available and staffed
- ◆ Survey Data
  - Parents
  - Staff
  - Students
- ◆ Teacher and Staff Data
  - Number of new staff
  - Positions still to be filled
  - Positions and special responsibilities of current staff
  - Special responsibilities still to be assigned or filled
  - Lists of teachers to be formally evaluated
  - Lists of staff on remediation or special circumstance
- ◆ School Improvement Plan (SIP)
  - Results from previous year

Template for the List of Data Sources for Your Initial Review: Current and Trend Data can be found at www.eyeoneducation.com.

Template 26. Data Analysis Handout:
A Guide to Asking Good Questions Together

A. Reviewing Student Learning Data

◆ As you review your student learning data, which curricular areas:

- Are stronger?
- Are weaker and potential targets for improvement?

◆ Which students are: (Consider AYP groupings and grade levels as a starting place)

- Performing well?
    - Percentage of students who met or exceeded proficiencies in specific content standards
    - Based on other measures
- Performing more poorly than peers?
    - Percentage of students scoring in the lower two performance levels
    - Based on other measures

◆ What are other relevant subgroups to consider given our school's demographics? What performance gaps exist between student groups?

- Ethnic groups
- Gender groups
- English Proficient and Limited English Proficient students
- Economically disadvantaged and other economic groups
- Other relevant subgroups

◆ What is:

- The distribution of scores across performance levels?
- The year-to-year progress of all students meeting or exceeding?
- The trend data in reducing the percentage of students in the bottom two levels?

B. Reviewing Other Important School Data

◆ As you review other important school data, what needs do you identify? (Discipline data, permitted students, drop-out rates, attendance, graduation rates, completer rates, etc.)

- What trends do you see?
- Are there unusual circumstances or specific initiatives that have impacted your data trends?
- Are there areas that you want to closely monitor over the next school year?
- Are there areas of greater urgency? What makes these areas more urgent to address than others?

C. Previous Year's School Improvement Plan (SIP)

◆ As you review the SIP in its entirety, what are the primary focus areas that were identified?

- Do these areas reflect areas that data supports as areas of need?
- What other considerations contributed to the selection of these areas of focus? (You may have to ask questions of your supervisor and/or staff to answer this question.)

- Were staff members, in your discussions over the summer, knowledgeable about the goal areas?
- ◆ In your review of student learning data:
  - What current data were used to determine the focus areas as needs and to monitor progress?
  - What other data are available and could be used?
  - If the results of last year's student achievement assessments are now available, have the goals of last year's SIP been met? If they have not been met, has progress been demonstrated?
  - Are there areas of this SIP that have not been met and should be continued in the next SIP?

D. *Draft* School Improvement Plan for the Upcoming School Year
- ◆ In the previous section, you may have listed goal areas of last year's SIP that were not met and should be continued. Are these areas reflected in the new SIP? If so:
  - Are the indicators in the new goal statement appropriate in light of last year's progress?
  - Are the activities for supporting the goal refined to obtain results or are they identical to last year's?
  - Do the new goal and activities reflect the student learning data? If not, what "tweaks" need to be considered?

  If not:
  - What changes in the draft plan need to be considered?
- ◆ Do the goal areas currently included in the draft SIP reflect areas that data supports as areas of need?
- ◆ Are there any other considerations that need to be reflected in your SIP for this upcoming year? (You may have to ask questions of your supervisor and/or staff to answer this question.)
- ◆ Who was included in the development of the draft SIP for the upcoming year and what process was decided upon to review the draft and finalize the plan?
  - Can the process be implemented? (Are the individuals available and willing?)
  - If it cannot be implemented, or no process was developed to finalize the SIP:
    - Determine who needs to be involved
    - Communicate with these individuals to identify time, needed resources and to use their knowledge of the building/staff/community to make certain that you are not overlooking someone who should be involved.
    - Develop and provide any materials/information/data needed by the group to facilitate your work together.

E. General
- ◆ What questions do you need to seek the answers to over the course of this upcoming school year?

Template for the Data-Analysis Handout can be found at www.eyeoneducation. com.

Planning for School Improvement

Districts have a variety of names for planning processes and documents that are used to initiate and sustain continuous improvement in their schools. The processes used, the format, the contents required, and the timelines for improvement planning also may vary and are generally influenced by the district's strategic plan and accreditation requirements from the state. There are, however, many similarities. In general:

- The current year's SIP usually is due to the district during the first few weeks of the school year. Meaningful student achievement improvement goals are difficult to generate without the results of last year's assessments, which may not be accessible until late summer.

- Most schools begin thinking about next year's goals in the spring of the calendar year.

- No Child Left Behind legislation has defined the degree to which schools are expected to improve student achievement results. There is little or no wiggle room here. The greatest flexibility schools have is in *how* they will achieve the expected results.

- Accountability and accreditation legislation in most states requires the involvement of non–staff members in the development of improvement goals and the monitoring of progress schools are making.

- The movement of many schools toward collaborative learning communities has implications for the degree of involvement of staff members and others in the development of school improvement initiatives.

The bottom line here is that there are significant expectations of schools and their leaders to assure continuous student gains in achievement. Leading this effort is an awesome responsibility. There are strategies that principals can use to simplify the processes used, the information flow, and the tools used to create, monitor, and report on SIPs.

The following pages include typical timelines, associated tasks, suggested processes, and tools that can be used in school improvement planning, monitoring, and reporting.

Timelines for School Improvement Planning

To Do Now

- If you are not aware of your district's timelines, contact your supervisor immediately for a timeline that also lists associated tasks and district expectations.

♦ As you study this document, *now* is the time to take stock of the status of your school's work related to district expectations and task completion.

♦ Investigate and identify what groups have been involved in the process of school improvement planning to date. During your first year in a school, we suggest that you capitalize on the knowledge of those who have been involved in the process and, over the course of the year, make decisions about any changes or "tweaks" that need to be made in these processes or membership.

♦ Establish a meeting date with those involved in the improvement planning process.

♦ Use your analysis of the most recent student assessment data and other current school data from pages 168 and 169. Summarize your analysis in a document, or compile appropriate documents that can be easily used and understood by those who are working with you on the SIP. Information that we suggest you include is listed below:

  • The results of last year's SIP goals

  • Achievement trend data

  • Any other school data that has a connection with the draft goals. *A list of possible data sources is given on page 167.*

  • A copy of the guiding questions (pages 168 and 169) that you can use to help your planning team discuss the available data.

  • A copy of the district timelines, expectations, and associated tasks.

Prior to School Improvement Plan Due Date

♦ Prior to the first meeting, distribute the information you have compiled to your planning team with a cover memo and the first meeting agenda. A sample cover memo that includes the agenda (Template 27, page 173) is included for you.

♦ During your first meeting, establish a calendar that will allow:

  • The team to finalize the goals.

  • Time for appropriate staff to review the activities in which they are involved that support the goals. Activities that support the goals usually are developed in grade-level teams or departments.

  • Time to review the plan by any other group from which approval of the plan is required per your district guidelines, for example, the Building Accountability Committee.

- Review of the completed document by any district official from whom a signature is required.

Implementing the School Improvement Plan

As the school year progresses, you and your planning team have three additional important issues with which to deal. These questions should be raised at the beginning of the year so that clearly identified goals and processes are established:

♦ How will you and your staff monitor the school's progress on the new plan throughout the year?

♦ How will you and your staff make decisions about adjustments in the plan during the year if monitoring data suggest that adjustments are needed?

♦ What information or training does your staff need to fully implement the SIP and the activities that support it?

Template 27. Memorandum

To: School Improvement Planning Team
From: Principal Name
Date
Re: Preparing for our Meeting

　　　Thank you all again for agreeing to continue working on our School Improvement Planning this year! I have so much to learn from you and to learn with you as we work through this process together! As we agreed, we will be meeting at 3:00 PM on Tuesday, September 7 in the Media Center. In order to value your time and thoughtful approach to our work, I have compiled both a tentative agenda and the reference materials we will need to continue the work you have invested so heavily in. Anything that requires advance attention on our part in order to maximize our meeting productivity is indicated in bolded print.

　　　Please review the tentative agenda below. If you have suggestions to improve it, please let me know as soon as possible.

Tentative Agenda

Meeting Outcomes:
- Understanding of history and roles in the school improvement plant (SIP) work to date
- Applying district timelines, expectations, and guidelines to our work
- Begin analyzing the draft goals' alignment with past goals, results, and current data
- Establish next meeting date, agenda, and responsibilities prior to meeting

I.　Team member introductions
- Role and responsibilities in process to date

II.　Review of district timelines, expectations, and guidelines
- How does our work to date conform to district expectations and guidelines?
- What is missing? How will we address these gaps?
- Establish our meetings and projected tasks based on district timelines

III.　Team dialog based on review of documents provided in advance
- What results do we show on last year's SIP?
- Which students are performing well? Which students are not?
- Do our draft goals reflect needs from last year's SIP and our current data? Why or why not?

IV.　4:10 PM: Progress check, planning, and closure
- To what degree have we accomplished our meeting outcomes?
- What agenda items do we need to include at our next meeting?
- What advance work will that require of our team?
- Is there anything we need to change to increase our meeting productivity?

V.　Notes:　Next Meeting Date:_____

Next Meeting's Agenda Items:　　　　　　　Responsibilities Prior to Next Meeting:

_____　　　　　_____

_____　　　　　_____

_____　　　　　_____

The following information has been attached for your thoughtful review in preparation for our meeting:

- Last year's SIP and results
- Current achievement data and other pertinent school data
- Guiding questions to help you review the SIP and data
- District documents: timeline, expectations, guidelines

Thanks so much!!

　　　Template for the Memorandum can be found at www.eyeoneducation.com for your modification.

Designing Your First Staff Meeting

As you have become more familiar with your new school, you have begun to identify and list topics you feel are essential to start-up. This initial list is your pre-planning list. Now it is time to *Plan!*

As you start the planning process, consider this information from Community at Work, a think tank and consulting firm. They suggest that an overcrowded agenda, filled with topics for which purposes have not been made clear, causes the participants to be frustrated and confused. The participants are unable to distinguish clear messages or priorities. Sam Kaner, working in cooperation with Community at Work in the his book *Facilitator's Guide to Participatory Decision-Making* (1996), designed a simple process to finalize agenda topics. His illustration appears below:

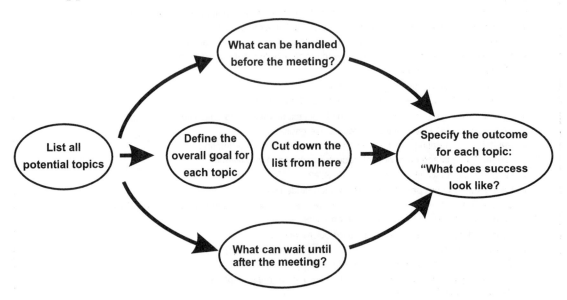

An overcrowded agenda undermines a group's ability to think intelligently. To prevent that from happening, invest a little time following the steps listed in Kaner's illustration.

Considerations as You Design Your First Staff Meeting Agenda

♦ *Context of the Agenda*

This is the first staff meeting of the year. Staff members have not seen each other for a long time, and they will take care of their social and relationship needs regardless of your tightly timed and sequenced agenda. You will need to build time prior to the actual start of the meeting for people to visit. You can plan for this by having a breakfast for them 30 minutes prior to the meeting, including topics for group discussion as a warm-up and grounding activity.

♦ *Time of Day, Meeting Place, and Energy of the Staff*

- Generally speaking, staff have far greater energy in staff meetings that occur prior to having invested a day with students. The earlier in the day that a meeting can occur, the better!

- The meeting place is important. If everyone is sitting on hard benches at cafeteria tables, attention soon will reduce considerably. Make certain you select an area, or arrange an area (if you have only one place large enough for the entire staff), to maximize potential for accomplishing your meeting outcomes. For example, if you are going to do small group work, set up tables and chairs that are appropriate for that activity and will not waste time in rearrangement during the meeting.

♦ *Sequence of Topics*

- Vary activities throughout the meeting to maximize engagement.

- Conduct activities that require critical thinking early in the meeting.

- Information-only topics can be last. They require little thought. Be sure to include a reference sheet in case minds have shut down at that point.

♦ *Best Practices*

- Several sources for staff meeting practices and staff development models are included in your bibliography. Take advantage of these resources to help you identify strategies for highly engaging and active meetings.

- Think of each meeting's agenda as being part of a larger picture. What happened at the last meeting? How will the agenda position the group for the future? What will the next meeting(s) look like? Careful planning prior to every meeting allows the principal to identify outcomes and to role model effective practices that actively engage participants and result in accomplishing meeting outcomes.

- Part of every meeting agenda can include identifying work that can be accomplished by group members between meetings. It may include research, editing, distributing minutes, seeking input from others, and analyzing an idea. Using this strategy can reduce the tendency to overload an agenda.

An example of a first staff meeting agenda follows (Template 28, page 176). An example for agenda development appears in Template 29 (page 178).

Template 28. First Staff Meeting Agenda (Example)

XYZ School
First Staff Meeting
Date/7:30 AM—in the Courtyard first!

Agenda

I.	Breakfast and Welcome in the Courtyard	Principal Name	7:30
	Reconnecting! Welcome Back!! After eating, please move to the library and sit with your team. Tables have been arranged, and your materials are on your tables. Please be ready to begin our meeting at 8:30. Coffee, tea, and bottled water are available for you on your way in.		
II.	**_Connecting and Celebrating_**	Principal, Team Leaders	8:30
	■ Meeting our new staff ■ Meeting staff with new responsibilities ■ 5, 10, 20, 25, and, 30 year recognitions		
III.	A Message from (Principal): Where are we? Where are we going?		
	Learning, Challenges, Planning ■ Summer interviews and work ■ Cluster meeting with the superintendent: his focus ■ Our School improvement Plan (SIP) ■ Our challenges ■ Our priorities 　● Staff Activity: School Climate		
IV.	Updates		
	Having the Information and Materials You Need for Start-up ■ Facility and facility staff ■ Opening schedule/first day for students ■ Study hall supervision/student IDs—changes ■ Data processing ■ Staff training/laptop upgrades	Assistant Principal Assistant Principal Assistant Principal Responsible Staff Member Technology Staff	
	The remainder of the staff updates are provided for you on a "Staff Information Sheet" and will be reviewed in your Team Meetings. Please see one of the administrators or your Team Leader if you have questions on any of the information.		
V.	Announcements		
	■ Superintendent's sounding boards ■ Committee involvement ■ Team meetings ■ Social/courtesy	■ Parking ■ Staff social—Friday ■ Teachers' Association news ■ Other	
VI.	Questions and Closure		10:30
	Clarifying and Bringing This Work to a Close		

Template for the First Staff Meeting Agenda can be found at www.eyeon education.com and on page 177.

Template 28. First Staff Meeting Agenda

_____ **School**
First Staff Meeting

Agenda

I.	Breakfast and Welcome	Principal Name	Time:
II.	_**Connecting and Celebrating**_	Principal, Team Leaders	
III.	A Message from (Principal): Where are we? Where are we going?		
IV.	Updates		
V.	Announcements		
VI.	Questions and Closure		10:30

Template 29. Agenda Development

Group: First Staff Meeting			Date: August 28, 2006	
Time: 8:00 AM			Location: Library	
Estimated Time	*Topic*	*Outcome*	*Strategy/Materials*	*Notes*
1 hour	Breakfast Welcome	Reconnecting	Relaxed location Start-up packets	Catered meal

Notes for follow-up:

Next Meeting: **Possible Topics:**

Template for Agenda Development can be found at www.eyeoneducation.com for your modification.

Chapter Summary

In order to ensure that school renewal is supported, you have reviewed and developed methods for monitoring the school's progress. You have assessed the ways in which people are heard in your building and the ways in which they influence decisions made in your building. You have created effective forums for people to work together. You have carefully analyzed the variety of ways decision-making happens, and you have been deliberate in your use of decision-making models in your school. Finally, you have come to understand your school's strengths and its areas of need. By doing so, you have been able to communicate to your stakeholders the goals to sustain school renewal and have begun to draft a school improvement plan that will move your school forward.

10

Accomplishment: Sustaining Family and Community Partnerships

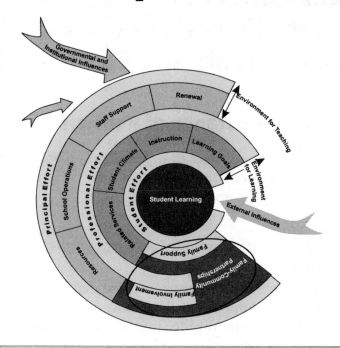

Essential Tasks

Identifying the Value Messages You Want to Convey

Examining Current Practices that Promote Family Support

Preparing for Your First Communications With Parents

Planning Student–Parent Orientations

Parent–Community Groups' Initial Meetings

Planning and Implementing a Successful Open House

10

Sustaining Family and Community Partnerships

Examining Current Practices and Initiating Effective Communication With Parents and Community

The Importance of Partnerships

When we consider the importance of strong family–community partnerships, we need to look at two different perspectives:

♦ What are families doing that *directly supports* the learning of their own children?

♦ How are families and community partners *involved* in the school to support the learning of all children?

All of us have seen schools that invest a great deal of time just trying to get families and community to support students and the school in any capacity. We also know of schools where community members, businesses, and families are active in and committed to the school and students. Both ends of this spectrum have their own set of challenges. Productive relationships between the school and families, community members, and organizations can foster the school's mission and promote initiatives and practices that accelerate student learning, the aim for all of us.

The development of productive relationships between the school and families/community members is fostered by open and honest communications, behaviors that demonstrate mutual respect, and a consistent focus on productive adult actions that impact student learning.

Immediately upon your appointment, parents and community members wonder how you, as the new principal, will work with them and with their children. They wonder how things will be different or to what degree things will remain as they know them. Their first impression of you, what you stand for, and the messages you give them will contribute to developing healthy relationships that will benefit the children in your school—or not. The degree to which you develop productive relationships with families and community members will establish the foundation for their involvement.

This chapter includes strategies and activities that will allow you to:

- Identify the consistent value messages that you want to convey to families and community partners in all communications/forums (Template 30, page 184)

- Identify *current* practices that promote family support of each student and *current* practices that involve families and community partners in the school to support the learning of all students

- Identify possible start-up forums/communications with parents and community partners that are opportunities to convey the messages you have identified

- Consider possible strategies for communications prior to the school year

- Develop initial communications using examples as a starting place and then modifying them to meet your needs

Prior to, or very early in the school year, it is important that time be taken to reflect on accomplishments and priorities for action during "start-up" and as the year unfolds. This activity frames your reflection in terms of *legitimacy*. It will require you to clearly define what it is you value and to align your actions and verbal messages with those values. It does not mean that everyone takes on your values. It does mean that they know that your values guide your thinking and actions. When this is true, those you work with, whether they are parents, staff, students, community, or colleagues, can predict actions you will take in a given circumstance. This means that there are relatively few *"surprises."* As a result, they can *trust* you. One definition of *trust* is the ability of those around you to predict your actions in any given circumstance. This is critical in initiating and building productive working relationships and fosters a sense of legitimacy in your work. All those you work with will immediately begin to paint a picture of you as a leader through the messages, actions, and interactions you have during your first few days and years as a principal. Being very clear with yourself and with others about your values and assuring the translation of your values into actions is a first step in initiating and building a productive environment for teaching and for learning in your school.

Template 30. Identifying the Value Messages You Want to Convey

What do I want people to understand that I believe in and stand for?

List the values that are priorities for you and that you want others to see translated into action during your tenure.

Example: I value the expertise of others.

_____

_____

_____

_____

_____

_____

_____

_____

_____

_____

_____

_____

Instilling Confidence

How will you translate your value messages into actions that instill confidence of these stakeholders in your credibility as their principal?

List other behaviors that you believe will instill confidence in you as principal

- Coherence between language and actions

- Willingness to learn

- Working tone

- Expectations of self and others

- Understanding/ respecting the past: icons, heroes and rituals

- • • • • • • • •

Critical Start-Up Responsibilities

Critical start-up responsibilities done well List the critical start-up tasks that will be opportunities to convey your value messages to these stakeholders

1. Summer contacts with parents/community partners

2. Parent and Student orientations

3. Open House

4.

5.

Values to Actions—Translation

How will you translate your value messages into actions that instill confidence of stakeholders in your credibility as their principal?

List actions below

Ex: I value the expertise of others

- Ask parents/ community partners to describe current practices that support student learning

- Include parent/ community partners who chair committees (PTA, Building Accountability Advisory Committee [BAAC], etc.) in planning start-up meetings

Template Identifying the Value Messages You Want to Convey can be found at www.eyeoneducation.com and on pages 186–187.

Template 30. Identifying the Value Messages You Want to Convey

What do I want people to understand that I believe in and stand for?

List the values that are priorities for you and that you want others to see translated into action during your tenure.

Instilling Confidence

How will you translate your value messages into actions that instill confidence of these stakeholders in your credibility as their principal?

List other behaviors that you believe will instill confidence in you as principal

_____

Critical Start-Up Responsibilities

Critical start-up responsibilities done well
List the critical start-up tasks that will be opportunities to convey your value messages to these stakeholders

_____

1.

2.

3.

4.

5.

Values to Actions—Translation

How will you translate your value messages into actions that instill confidence of stakeholders in your credibility as their principal?

List actions below
Ex: I value the expertise of others

_____

Examining Current Practices
That Promote Family Support

Definition

Family support activities encourage and promote student effort. Family/community support might involve, for example, providing encouragement for academic work, creating a quiet place to study, making sure students come to school with everything they need, and communicating that school work has higher priority than television, extra hours on community jobs, or recreation.

In the *Framework for School Leadership Accomplishments*, family–community partnerships comprise the full range of strategies through which the school shares responsibility for children's growth and learning with families and other community groups.

Why Are Family–Community Partnerships Important?

Students spend only a small fraction of their time in school. If student effort is to be sufficient to reach ambitious learning goals, schools need allies in supporting student effort. Parents, employers, and other community leaders are potentially important allies. In fact, the rewards, encouragement, and sanctions that parents and community members can use to support student effort often are much more powerful than those available to the school.

What Systems Are Currently in Place
Within Your School to Promote Family Support?

Brainstorm a list of all systems currently in place. Template 31 (page 189) provides several categories that may spur your thinking.

Template 31. Systems in Our School
That Promote Family Support (Example)

Programs	Information	Communications	Special Events—In School
Example: Homework Hotline	*Example:* Parent Link (Online access to daily attendance records and grades)	*Example:* Parent Power Column in Newsletter	Example: Family Literacy Nights

Template for Systems in Our School that Promote Family Support can be found at www.eyeoneducation.com and on page 190.

Template 31. Systems in Our School
That Promote Family Support

Programs	Information	Communications	Special Events— In School

Questions to Guide Your Thinking

1. Are there areas that currently have limited supports in place? If so, how will you gather ideas to fill those gaps during the course of the year?

2. Do you currently have access to data that give you information about how these supports are valued/utilized?

   • List possible strategies for gathering that data.

3. Once you have this data, how will you use it to improve systems that promote parent support?

4. Do you need to include any of these support systems in communications prior to the beginning of the school year? Which ones? How will you accomplish that?

   Example: Lists of needed school supplies must be included in the August newsletter.

Preparing for Your First Communications With Parents

We are all aware of the importance of first impressions. The first connection with a person, whether it is through a letter, phone call, or personal meeting, creates impressions that stay with us for a long time to come. From that first interaction, we make judgments about that person and how we believe she/he will behave in the future. That is why you want to be thoughtful about your first communications with parents.

When a parent meets you, talks with you on the phone, or reads a letter sent home to them with their child, what do you want their *impressions* to be? How do you want that parent to *describe* you?

♦ Respectful
♦ Concerned
♦ Approachable
♦ Friendly
♦ Energetic
♦ Willing to listen and take time for me
♦ Solution oriented
♦ Committed to my child's safety and success

These are often the behaviors that parents tell us they want to experience when communicating with their child's principal. Feel free to adopt this list, if it works for you, or to add, delete, and modify this list to design your "ideal impressions," but create a list of descriptors that allows you to regularly evaluate your communications against how you want to be perceived. Some principals keep this list in a visible place on their desk, as a reminder when talking on the phone or meeting with parents in their office. Soon it becomes internalized. Let's explore how these impressions get built into different settings.

Phone Calls

1. The tone of your voice upon the "first hello" speaks volumes to the person on the other end of the line. Is it friendly and inviting? Can they *hear you smiling* through the phone? Or is it abrupt and rushed? "Good morning. This is Ryan Brooker. How may I help you?" using an upbeat and friendly tone of voice is significantly more positive than an all business tone "Mr. Brooker." When greeted warmly, even callers with a complaint get the message immediately, "Hey, maybe I don't have to be rude. This person sounds like someone I can work with."

2. Take the time to hear what the parent is saying. Don't interrupt. Often, by trying to rush the conversation, you create new issues that require even more time to work through.

3. If you are initiating the call, be sure to inquire whether this is a good time to talk. Do they have a few minutes to visit with you?

4. Summarize the conversation, ensuring that you both are in agreement as to what has been decided.

5. If applicable, make note of the follow-up actions you said you would take.

6. Call your own message machine. See how your voice sounds and what your message implies. If it isn't a message that you would like to receive as a caller, re-record your message.

7. Build into your schedule at least three "sunshine calls" per week, that is, calls to parents telling them something positive about their child. It will make their day and yours, too!

8. At the same time that you are monitoring your phone etiquette, you will want to monitor how your school phone is answered by office personnel. They are your representatives. If you have an automated system, is it helpful and efficient? Or does it create confusion and frustration for the caller before they even reach a real person? If it isn't caller friendly, redesign your system.

Personal Meetings and Interactions

1. Create regular opportunities to have informal contact with the parents of your students. Let them know, for example, that you will be on the playground every morning for 15 minutes before the bell rings. Wave and initiate greetings.

2. Be sure to acknowledge parents that you see in the office or in the hallways. Too often, we have heard parents say, "She walked right past me and didn't even say hello." It is easy to do this when we have a number of things on our minds, but you will want to create an awareness of who is around you, even when you are busy. People are often offended by this simple lack of acknowledgment.

3. When meeting with a parent in your office, make sure that your office arrangement allows for you to come from behind your desk and sit with them in comfortable chairs without barriers. Staying behind your desk creates distance and a sense of unequal power.

4. Offer the same courtesies to a parent coming to your office that you would to a guest in your home. Shake their hands and offer them some water, coffee, or tea.

5. Be aware of your voice tone and body language. Those messages are much stronger than anything that you will say.

6. If warranted, take notes on the key issues you are discussing. This assures you of an accurate recording and tells the parent that you are taking this discussion seriously.

7. There may be times when parents stop in and you are in the process of reading or writing something. As tempting as it might be to finish your work, stop! You will be sending the message, "I'm really too busy to see you now." No one wants to be given that message.

Written Messages
(Letters, Newsletter Columns, Reminders, etc.)

1. As a general rule, always begin your written communication with a personal greeting before going directly to content. Again, you want to come across as welcoming and friendly.

2. Subscribe to the 30-3-30 Rule: 80% of the parents will spend just 30 seconds reading what you send home; 19% will spend just 3 minutes; and 1% will spend 30 minutes (and that's *your* mother!) Be clear, be concise, be courteous! (From *127 Ideas Principals Can Use Now to Build a Successful Parent Involvement Program*. Presentation by John H. Wherry, Presi-

dent, The Parent Institute, Fairfax Station, Virginia, at the 1997 NAESP Convention, San Antonio, Texas, March 14, 1997.)

3. Whenever possible, have a set day that parents can expect written communications from you and their teachers ("Take Home Tuesdays" for example). Students will be more likely take them out of the backpacks and parents will be more likely to read them.

4. *Proofread* and then *proofread* again! Typos, and spelling and grammar errors really irritate people, especially when they come from educators. They also send the message that you are someone who doesn't attend to detail, not a quality they want to see in a principal.

5. A Letter of Introduction (Template 32, page 195) is one model for a welcome letter.

Template 32. Letter of Introduction/Welcome Back to School

Dear Families of Martin Luther King Elementary School,

On behalf of all of the staff at Martin Luther King Elementary School, it is indeed my pleasure to welcome you to a new and exciting school year. For those of you whose children have attended our school in the past, we are so glad to have you returning. And for those of you whose children are just entering King, we are pleased to have you as a part of our school community.

Let me also take this opportunity to introduce myself. My name is Roger Docker, and I am honored to be serving as your new principal. Although I have had the pleasure of meeting with some of you last spring during the interview process and with others as you stopped by the school this past summer, I look forward to meeting each of you very soon. My family and I have lived in Colorado Springs for the past nine years, and previously I served as a literacy coordinator at Woods Elementary School while working on my principal licensure. One of my children, Sarah, will be attending school here at King, while my other two children, Jason and Tad, will be students at Carver Middle School. My wife, Betsy, is a school nurse at Cleveland High School, so we are clearly a District #70 family.

I know from meeting with teachers, parents, community members, and your past principal, Tom Langley, that King is a school committed to excellence. Academic achievement, character development, commitment to safety, and a sense of belonging and community are clearly high priorities at King. Please be assured of my commitment to honoring your accomplishments and my hope of contributing to even greater success in the future.

In the spirit of building community, let me invite each of you to the Open House sessions being held next week at our school. Attached you will find a flyer providing all of the details. Count on seeing a tall man with a green necktie near the front door to greet you—that would be me ready to shake your hand.

Our first newsletter will be sent home on Tuesday in your child's "Take Home Tuesday Mail Folder." Plan to take some time reviewing the newsletter, as it will provide you with important information regarding upcoming events, classroom updates, and parent and community activities.

Again, I want to welcome all of you to what we hope will be your best school year yet. Please do not hesitate to stop by the office or to give us a call if we can assist you in any way. Best wishes to you and your family, and "Go Trailblazers!"

Sincerely,

Template for the Letter of Introduction/Welcome Back to School can be found at www.eyeoneducation.com for your modification.

August Newsletter

Although you may have had the opportunity to meet a few parents, it is very important that you communicate with *all* parents prior to the beginning of the school year. Parents of students who are new to the school have all kinds of questions about the school and its operations. They want to have information so that both they and their student are prepared for school to begin. Parents of students who are continuing at your school still need start-up information, but they also are interested in you. Will new leadership bring changes in practices to which they are accustomed? *All* parents care about the leadership of their children's school. Who is this new principal, and do we have enough information to have confidence in her/his leadership?

What Do I Need to Include in the August Newsletter?

- ◆ A message from the principal: brief, clear, positive, and focused on the school, what you have learned from stakeholders about the school, and student achievement. A sample Principal's Message (Template 33, page 198) is included.
- ◆ Parent–student orientation information
- ◆ Registration information
- ◆ Class schedule information (secondary); class list information (elementary)
- ◆ School supplies lists
- ◆ Bus schedule
- ◆ Start-up schedule
- ◆ Field trip policies/practices
- ◆ Lunch information
- ◆ Testing information related to new students and start-up
- ◆ Updates on staffing, enrollment, and facility upgrades
- ◆ School picture information
- ◆ Student identification information
- ◆ List of school resources and telephone numbers
- ◆ Sports and/or intramural information
- ◆ Parking information (secondary)
- ◆ Open house information
- ◆ Safety information
- ◆ School calendar

- Newsletter, progress report, and report card distribution dates
- Calendar of events for August and September
- A "Parent Power" column: helping your student organize for learning at school and at home

The start-up newsletter usually is large. For that reason, it needs to be organized in a way that parents are provided with the important information they need, priorities are clear, and the format allows parents to pull out reference pages for refrigerator posting. If you have enough information to include a "Kudos" section to recognize adults and students for achievements, awards, or effort, do it! Thanks and recognitions are an important part of any newsletter.

Newsletter Tips

- Become familiar with mass mailing procedures.
- Become familiar with procedures for having your newsletter compiled, printed, and prepared for mailing. Timing is critical. All schools in your district are trying to publish and mail newsletters at the same time you are. Make certain that you have allowed enough time.
- Be sure to mail the newsletter at least two weeks prior to the beginning of school. Using the student start date, count backward on the calendar for all timelines (number of days for compilation, editing, printing, preparing for mailing, and mail delivery). This will give you deadlines for each step in the publishing and distribution process.
- Check, double check, and triple check the accuracy of the newsletter. Format, grammar, and content are very important. Parents will make judgments about your competency based on the information they have. Because you are just beginning, the newsletter is the only piece of information that most of them have about you.
- Make a checklist of all topics you need to include. Double check that they are included *prior* to printing. This is not the time for an "oh well..." approach.

Make sure that the format is reader friendly, welcoming, and informative. Have someone else read it prior to publication. Make any needed changes.

As you are developing the newsletter content, go back to the value messages that you identified earlier in this chapter. Does the content of your newsletter reflect those messages?

Template 33. Principal's Message/Back to School Newsletter

Welcome to the new school year! We are excited about having your student as a part of the (School) community and are committed to providing the best educational opportunities possible. We all look forward to an outstanding school year!

As a newcomer, I value the summer opportunity to meet with each staff member and with many parents, students, alumni, and members of the business community. You will be as pleased as I am, I think, to hear that each group identified the same priorities and listed similar topics as challenges that we face this year. That says a great deal about the high level of communication within our school community!

♦ Identified as the greatest strength of this fine school is **the reputation of excellence** that reflects the broad spectrum of educational opportunities to support individual student needs and that inspires the confidence of the school community. Second, the school community values the atmosphere of the school where **uniqueness and diversity of all individuals are embraced and are essential to the integrity of the central mission of the school.** You all have asked that I protect and promote these essential qualities of our school. I pledge to you that I will.

♦ Identified as challenges we face this year are **implementing the state-level assessment program that includes Individual Literacy Plans (ILPs) for students who are not proficient in reading** in a way that promotes achievement of our students and is understood by our community, completion of our **facility projects,** and **continued improvement in the condition of the facility**.

These strengths and challenges are priorities for us and are related to the goals of our School Improvement Plan, which maintains our primary focus on each student's achievement. I will update you on all of these topics at **Open House on September ( ).** Musical entertainment will begin in the auditorium at 6:45 PM, and the program will start at 7:00 PM. Please come early to enjoy the musical program. That evening, you will have the opportunity to visit with your student's teachers about curriculum, class procedures, and expectations.

Your active participation in your student's education is the singular most critical factor in her/his achievement. It promotes student attendance and a focus on studies, and it reinforces the importance of achievement and education. Parents as partners with the school send a very clear message to their students that learning matters. There are many ways to be involved, and we will explain those to you at Open House.

On a personal note, I want to thank the entire (School) community for the warm and supportive reception that I have received. I am so pleased to be here! I am committed to making your experience in this special school a positive one, too! I am excited about being part of a school community that celebrates a long standing **tradition of excellence!**

If at any time during the year you have questions or concerns, please call me or stop by.

See you soon,

Principal
E-mail address/Phone number

Template for the Principal's Message/Back to School Newsletter can be found at www.eye oneducation.com for your modification.

Other Written Communications from the School

Schools can use a variety of flyers or brochures to publicize events, send home reminders, or describe the school program. Principals are encouraged to consider a number of factors before they approve the effort and expense associated with written documents to send home. Some of these considerations are:

- *What is the purpose of this communication?* Are you showcasing a special program to draw enrollment or simply reminding parents of their conference time? Determining the purpose will guide your decisions about color versus black-and-white copy, quality of paper, and investment of staff time in development of the document.

- *Are there more effective ways to communicate this information to families?* For instance, could a volunteer parent from each classroom call the home of every student in the class to remind parents of conference dates and times?

- *How will the document be distributed?* Are you relying on students to get the paper home? What percentage of student-delivered mail really gets into parents' hands? How important is it that *every* parent receives the document? These answers will guide distribution choices.

Paper communications are not the only way to inform people. An overload of paper is a frustration for many. Be thoughtful in your choices about informing your community.

Other Communication Strategies for Information Sharing

Schools have become proactive and creative in finding new ways to communicate with their communities for a variety of reasons. Some schools want to increase ways that parents are informed. Others want to find more cost-effective methods or simply more effective strategies. Before making the decision to develop *more* systems, it is important to consider the current systems and how well they are accomplishing the purposes intended. You have developed a list of communications systems in place at your school. You used guiding questions to develop an impression about the value and degree of utilization of the systems in place. In all cases, look first to systems that are in place and see if small changes in those systems would accommodate the need. If they will not, you will need to explore other options. The ideas below speak to factors you need to take into consideration and process steps that can be taken.

If you need to develop additional communication strategies, first determine the specific purpose of the communication needed.

Do parents want to be able to access attendance records daily? Do they need to have a more immediate way to check grades than quarterly report cards or grade checks? Are parents needing event information that is not available in the newsletter?

After determining the purpose, list possible strategies. For example:

To provide more immediate access to attendance, an online attendance system with parent passwords might work.

Determine how realistic the idea is and weigh the costs and the benefits. Talk to staff who would be involved in implementing the system. What ideas do they have? What resources are available in the district that would support development of this strategy?

Planning Student–Parent Orientations

Student–parent orientations are generally held just a few days prior to the beginning of school. Often there are several sessions so that parents can find one to attend. Two typical purposes of orientations are to provide information for families and to help students and parents to feel comfortable and welcome. Additional purposes may include:

- Completing paperwork
- Finalizing schedules
- Providing a transition from a previous school/home to a new school
- Getting parents into the school
- Completing needed assessments
- Relationship building between families and school personnel

It is important to establish your purpose(s) prior to building an agenda for the orientation. Identifying the purpose will help the principal and involved staff to list the topics that need to be included and can assist them in making decisions about strategies in presentation and materials. It also may be useful for the principal to review Identifying the Value Messages You Want to Convey (Template 30), as you begin identifying orientation purposes, topics to include and agenda development. The principal will need to find ways to include the value messages in orientation materials/presentation.

A planning template for Student–Parent Orientation Planning (Template 34, page 201) is included to assist in planning for this very important event.

Template 34. Planning for Student–Parent Orientation
(Example)

Orientation Purposes
■ Provide information for families. ■ Help students and parents to feel comfortable and welcome. Complete paperwork. ■ Provide an opportunity for relationship building between families and school personnel. ■ Initiate Link Crew support program for incoming freshmen.

Topics to Include for Parents

School Data	Supports for Students	Communication with families	Start-Up Information	School Expectations
■ School Data How do students in this school perform? • Achievement and performance trends • ACT/SAT • Graduation rate • Graduates next steps	■ Supports for Students How will my student get help and support? • Counselor • Ninth-grade support team • Peer counselors • Teachers	■ Communication with families How will I know how my student is doing at school? Who do I contact if I need help or questions answered? • Online access to attendance records/grades • Timelines and distribution of progress reports/grades/newsletter • List of school contacts (call anytime) • Conferences • Parent handbook	■ Start-Up Information How will the school year begin? What do I need to know to prepare my student? • First day schedule • Administrative meeting with students • Materials needed • Class schedule • School calendar	■ School Expectations What are the rules? What structure/systems are in place to provide direction for my student? How am I included in this? • Student handbook • Dress code • Attendance procedures • Parent questions and concerns?

Value Messages	**Agenda Ideas**

■ Student learning is the focus of all work.
■ Family involvement and support is critical to student learning.
■ We value the expertise of others.
	■ Begin with parents and students together
	• You are part of an exemplary school
	   • Data, awards, programs, pride
	   • Support systems
	■ Separate students and parents
	• Pair students with Peer Counselors and support team members; send them off.
	   • Relationship-building activities, student handbook, lockers, schedules, finding classrooms, food.
	• Parents receive information topics in PowerPoint format with a packet of reference info and handbook.
	   • Divide parents into groups with staff and counselors. Q and A sessions—relationship building, food

Template for Planning for Student–Parent Orientation can be found at www.eye oneducation.com and on page 201.

Template 34. Planning for Student–Parent Orientation

Orientation Purposes

-
-
-
-

Topics to Include for Parents

▪ School Data How do students in this school perform?	▪ Supports for Students How will my student get help and support?	▪ Communication with families How will I know how my student is doing at school? Who do I contact if I need help or questions answered?	▪ Start-Up Information How will the school year begin? What do I need to know to prepare my student?	▪ School Expectations What are the rules? What structure/systems are in place to provide direction for my student? How am I included in this?

Value Messages	*Agenda Ideas*
▪ ▪ ▪	

Parent—Community Groups' Initial Meetings

In Chapter 6 on Mobilizing Resources, you had an opportunity to take stock of parent organizations, booster groups, and other groups with community members in an advisory capacity to the school. In your analysis of those services, you developed a list of the groups and their primary contacts, and you have had meetings or phone conversations with the key contact people in these groups.

It is important that groups begin their work as early as possible in the new year. Commitments made at the beginning of the year are more likely to be sustained, and important team building occurs in the first few meetings. The most common parent and community groups that exist to support schools are:

- Parent—Teacher Organizations (PTOs)
- Booster Organizations
- Building Accountability Advisory Committees (BAACs)

The purpose of each of these groups is different. They are likely to operate differently, and the principal's role will vary in each group. Even if the principal's role is peripheral, her/his visibility at their events and meetings will make a statement that the principal values their efforts.

Parent—Teacher Organizations

Generally, PTOs are supportive in nature. The people who lead the group are parents, and the membership consists of parents, relatives, and supporters of the school. Usually, parents and others can belong to the organization by paying dues. The dues are one source of funding for the group to operate and to make donations to the school. Typically, many people are dues-paying members but only a few are the worker bees. Fundraisers and school projects are the primary work of these groups. Your relationship with those who are active and involved in the school is a priority. The more valued the active members feel and the more diligently you tend to these relationships, the greater the level of support from the organization for the school.

Booster Organizations

Booster organizations are common in schools. Two of the most common are band boosters and athletic booster's organizations. These groups operate to support specific programs in the school. They provide manpower for program events and often raise funds for the programs. The principal's role with these groups is similar to her/his role with PTOs.

Actions Principals Can Take
to Support the Work of Parent–Teacher Organizations
and Booster Organizations

- Building relationships and strong communication channels with active members
- Visibility during some part of the organization's events and meetings
- Availability to provide information about the school's needs
- Responding to requests of members in a timely way
- Remembering that the principal does not control these groups but does influence them
- Providing any district regulations and building procedures related to fundraising to the group and assuring compliance with those regulations
- Recognizing the organizations and specific member contributions in high-visibility ways

Building Accountability Advisory Committees

The BAAC is an organized, representative group that exists in an advisory role to the school. These groups have responsibilities that are most generally legislated and must work within regulation parameters defined by local Boards of Education. The committee is chaired by a parent or community member. The committee chair works closely with the principal. The principal is a member of the committee and is relied upon to provide information, answer questions, work collaboratively with the chairman to meet mandates, and serve as liaison with the staff at the school. The work of these committees becomes increasingly important as accreditation legislation is implemented by state governments. The principal does not control this committee but has a great deal of influence with the members and their work.

Actions Principals Can Take to Support
the Effective Work of Building Accountability
Advisory Committees

- Building relationships and strong communication channels with active members
- Providing information about the school's data, operations, programs, and budget
- Responding to requests of members in a timely way

- Recognizing the organizations and specific member contributions in high-visibility ways

- Providing training and information with the chairman for the group related to legislative, district, and building responsibilities and procedures

- Collaborating with the chairman on meeting agendas and information needed, and assuring that committee task responsibilities meet timelines

- Communicating effectively as the link between staff and the committee

First Meeting of the Building Accountability Advisory Committee

- Meet with the chairperson in advance of the meeting to establish the agenda and generate any needed materials. Important agenda items for the first meeting include:

  - Introductions as a grounding activity
  - Training related to legislated and district required responsibilities
  - Developing a year-long schedule of topics to be addressed to comply with responsibilities

- Direct your secretary to mail and e-mail meeting reminders with an agenda, at minimum, so that it arrives at least one week prior to the meeting.

- Provide a comfortable setting and food.

- Arrive early to the meeting to set up, organize materials, and personally greet each member.

- Allow the chairperson to run the meeting. Contribute as appropriate.

- Encourage participation of members by asking questions.

Accountability Committees can be a strong support for the principal in accomplishing the purposes and work of the school.

Planning and Implementing a Successful Open House

Inviting parents and families to an open house at the beginning of the school year has become a tradition in most schools. It is a formal way to welcome the significant others in your students' lives to the school and emphasize their role in the students' success.

You will likely want to begin by talking with staff members to determine the past norms for open house. Ask them to describe when these events typically were scheduled along with the format for the evening(s). Some questions you will want to ask:

- What was the date(s) and time(s) for last year's open house(s)?
- Was the open house scheduled to include all grade levels on the same evening, or were there several open houses over a 1- to 2-week period?
- Were students encouraged/expected to attend the open house with their parents?
- If students were to attend, did they receive clear expectations and coaching regarding entering the classroom, touring the building, introducing their family, etc.?
- What was the format? Did everyone begin the evening at a central location with the principal addressing the large group, or were they directed immediately to classrooms?
- Was there an agreed upon "agenda" for classroom teachers to follow in presenting pertinent information to parents?
- What printed materials were provided to the parents?
- Was the structure set up to simulate for parents the schedule of their students?
- How did parents have the opportunity to meet auxiliary staff members at the school?
- Was registration for PTO, school committees, Boys/Girls Scouts, etc., included in the open house?
- Were baby-sitting services provided for families with small children?
- Were refreshments provided?
- What were the expectations for displaying student work in the hallways and in the classrooms?
- How was the invitation to attend open house communicated? How far in advance? Were reminders used?
- Were students and/or adults stationed at certain locations in the building to welcome, direct, answer questions, etc.?
- Were your custodial or security staff available to ensure safety and support as needed?
- Was there a way for families to evaluate or provide feedback on the open house?

Once you have a good sense of what has occurred in the past, form an ad hoc committee, with representation from each grade level, team, or department, to discuss and finalize plans for this year's open house. Once all of the details are decided, ensure that all staff members are informed well in advance.

Throughout this book, we have discussed the importance of determining what messages you wish to send to your various audiences. Open house provides you and your staff with possibly one of the biggest audiences of the entire year and at a time when first impressions are critical. Talk with your staff about the key and consistent messages that you want to communicate throughout the evening by every staff member with whom parents or family members come in contact. Possible messages are:

- We are glad that you are here, and we consider you a vital member of the educational team.
- We are glad to have _____ in our school and in my classroom.
- Important learning goals that we have in this class are _____ _____.
- Behavioral and homework expectations are _____ _____.
- Grading policies are _____.
- Ways and frequency in which we will communicate with you are _____.
- Ways that you can most easily contact me are _____.
- Ways that you can support your student's success in school are _____.

When families leave your school following open house, how do you hope they describe you and your staff?

- Friendly
- Approachable
- Committed to all students' success
- Possesses a sense of humor
- Has high expectations for student learning and a support system for students to achieve
- Well organized
- Willing to problem solve issues

Whatever those descriptors are, check them against your plan for the open house and see if there are multiple opportunities to demonstrate these qualities and communicate these messages. Providing a brief evaluation for parents to complete at the end of the evening will contribute to making your next year's open house even more successful. We have provided a sample Open House Evaluation form (Template 35 on the following page).

Template 35. Open House Evaluation

_____ School
Open House Evaluation

Thank you so much for attending Open House! Your involvement is essential in our partnership to meet the learning needs of your student. Please take a moment as the evening ends to provide us with feedback on your Open House experience. We value your opinion! The results of this feedback will be summarized in the next newsletter and will be used to provide an even higher quality Open House next year.

Please use the ranking scale below rate your experience:

5 = Excellent

4 = Better than I had expected

3 = Average

2 = Less than I expected

1 = Unsatisfactory

5	4	3	2	1	
					The staff was friendly and approachable
					The evening was well organized
					The materials provided were clear, user-friendly, and understandable
					The Open House schedule allowed me to get needed information and to meet staff who work directly with my student
					I have information and references that will allow me to get help or information during the year from the school and staff
					The general information session was helpful and needed during Open House
					The meeting time with teachers was productive
					It is clear that our school has high expectations for student learning
					I am confident now that there are support systems in place to help students achieve

1. The best part of Open House was:

2. One suggestion I have to improve Open Houses in the future is:

3. Other comments:

Template for the Open House Evaluation can be found at www.eyeoneducation.com for your modification.

Chapter Summary

In order to ensure that family–community partnerships are supported, you have carefully examined the value messages you want to communicate to the community. After this reflection, you have examined the current practices in your building that promote family support. In order to build these relationships that are valuable to your school, you have carefully prepared for the various communications with parents. Phone conversations, personal meetings, and written messages all convey to the parents and community that their connection to the school is valued and important. You have carefully planned for successful student–parent orientations so that they are purposeful and meaningful occasions. In addition, you have helped other parent and community groups get off to a positive start of the year: parent–teacher organizations, booster groups, Building Accountability Committees, and other parent/community groups are off to a great start. Finally, a well-organized and informative open house allows parents to renew or establish their connection to the school. It is important to take all of these opportunities to allow parents and community members to participate in the school's activities, to connect to the school, and to feel valued and respected by the school's administration and staff.

Now that you have completed the reading about all of the Accomplishment Areas, it is time to finish your Entry Planner notes. Once you have done that, you can organize the tasks you need to complete by the month in which you need to attend to them. Use Template 2, Entry Planner Calendar of Tasks, to organize the responsibilities that you need to address. Start simply by organizing the responsibilities by month. Then, take it week by week. Remember, it is not necessary that you organize every week of the year right this minute. Organize important tasks for *this month* first. You will adjust your list and the target dates as time goes by. Most importantly, you will have your Entry Planner notes for reference and use throughout the year. How convenient, as compared to yet another stack of papers or sticky notes! Principals have enough to worry about without worrying that they might forget something important that requires their attention. This level of organization may seem vigorous. It is, but ultimately, it can free you from that worry and allow you to focus your full attention and energy on essential tasks at the appropriate time. Planning is critical to implementing well.

Appendix

Introduction to the Framework for School Leadership Accomplishments

The *Framework for School Leadership Accomplishments* (FSLA)[1] was developed to help principals and other school leaders manage the complexity of their jobs. School leaders work at the confluence of strongly held views about what schools should be like, what students should learn, what procedures work best, and how the responsibilities of families, teachers, and other community members should be balanced. Although principals' responsibilities raise big questions and have high stakes for each school community, the principal's daily work often feels more like an endless stream of small, unrelated problems.

Successful principals find ways of connecting large questions about purposes and results with the daily realities of life in schools. They use mental models (Senge, 1990) to understand their school's strengths and help decide which daily problems need attention and which ones can be left alone. Mental models can be as simple as a belief that the principal's job is to protect teachers from disruptions or as complex as an intricate theory of leadership or an understanding of the many ways that school operations affect teaching and learning.

The *Framework for School Leadership Accomplishments* is one mental model for school leadership. It evolved over several years in efforts to apply current research and theory in educational administration work with principals and school leadership teams who were engaged in the practical work of renewing their schools. The result is a distinctive way of thinking about school leadership that helps principals make the links between theory and reality and between school goals and daily problems.

The FSLA is unique in its use of *accomplishments* as the building blocks of the principal's role. Accomplishments are the conditions that principals and other school professionals try to create in their schools. For example, one way or

---

1   An earlier version of Appendix A appeared as Bellamy, T. (1999). *The whole school framework: A design for learning*. Oxford, OH: National Staff Development Council. Copyright G. T. Bellamy. Used with permission.

another, every school creates a climate for students, learning goals, schedules of activities, and so on. These school conditions, or accomplishments, are important for two reasons: (1) when developed effectively, they are the means through which the school supports student learning, and (2) when developed responsively, they express a collective vision of what school should be like. The principal's challenge, then, is to foster conditions in the school that promote student learning while also responding to community values about schools and schooling.

Accomplishments and School Leadership: Three Key Benefits

Why organize the work of school leaders around accomplishments? Certainly other ways of talking about school work are more familiar. For example, we often think of leadership in terms of the tasks to be done, the outcomes (student learning) to be achieved, the problems to be solved, and so on. Although each of these ways of framing the work of school leadership can help, we have chosen the idea of accomplishments because it seems to fit the special challenges of school leadership. As we use the term, *accomplishments* have three features that are particularly helpful.

Defining Quality Through Success Criteria

When many people first see the FSLA, they respond that learning goals, curriculum, student climate, and so on are indeed important parts of the school work but that the figure doesn't go far enough. Before supporting the framework, they want to know what kind of curriculum or climate we mean. The point is important. Most people automatically start adding modifiers to the accomplishments. For example, we want a climate that is welcoming, respectful of differences, challenging, friendly, and so on. These are the success criteria that define how well the school is doing with its student climate accomplishment and determine whether the climate will support or inhibit student learning.

Each school accomplishment becomes meaningful only when success criteria are defined. Some criteria come from research showing that some features of instruction or climate are related to student learning. Other success criteria reflect legal and ethical constraints on what a school can do. Still others come from the values and priorities of the principal, the school's staff, the students, and their families.

Thinking of accomplishments as having success criteria helps new principals in two ways. First, it emphasizes that leadership is about both ends and means. The principal must lead to build consensus about ends (What features are desired in the school's accomplishments?) as well as means (What needs to be done to realize accomplishments that meet those success criteria?). The second benefit relates to school assessment. Defining success criteria for all the school's accomplishments creates a yardstick for assessing how well the school is doing and provides a clear direction for improvement efforts.

Achieving Results Through Flexible Strategies

Accomplishments define the results achieved through a school's work, not the methods used to achieve those results. This means that the accomplishment perspective emphasizes *what* gets done rather than how it is achieved or who does it. For example, one accomplishment that supports student learning is the student climate that is sustained in the building. Climates can be developed and improved in many different ways. What is important is not which method was used (within some limits, of course), but whether the resulting climate is one that actually does support learning.

This emphasis on results instead of methods is important for new principals for at least three reasons. First, it avoids the suggestion that one right way exists for practically any task of school leadership. By emphasizing what gets done, the accomplishment perspective encourages a principal to be eclectic and to draw on information and ideas from many different sources. Second, the emphasis on results underscores just how different schools are from each other. No matter how well an approach worked elsewhere, it might or might not be useful in a principal's own school. Effective principals continuously study their school and community in order to understand the possibilities and constraints within which they work. Third, the emphasis on flexible methods encourages principals to share leadership widely. Who does the work is not as important as what gets accomplished.

Focusing on What the School Controls

The third benefit of the accomplishment perspective has to do with the reality of what we control and what we do not. Accomplishments are conditions and results over which the school has a reasonable level of control. Of course, there are many other influences on student learning that are outside the school's control. The *Framework for School Leadership Accomplishments* distinguishes two kinds of these external influences. The first, represented by the shaded portions of the figure on page 4, are the actions of individuals whom the school depends on to reach its goals and hopes to influence through its accomplishments. For example, the effort that students spend on their studies, the extra professional effort that teachers commit to their planning and learning, and the involvement of families in the learning process serve as critical links between the school's accomplishments and student learning.

The second kind of external influence includes the many, often very powerful, factors in the larger society that also influence student learning but over which the school exerts little or no control. For example, the attractiveness of television shows that compete with homework and the availability of health care and social services can profoundly affect learning but are beyond the school's control.

By distinguishing the accomplishments over which the school has at least some control, from the choices of participants, which the school tries to influence, and from the external factors, over which it has no effective control, the Framework helps to focus the school's efforts and maximize the impact of what it does control.

The Framework for School Leadership Accomplishments

The *Framework for School Leadership Accomplishments* identifies nine school accomplishments that, depending on how well they are achieved, influence the school's goal of student learning (see figure). In the figure, the nine accomplishments are arranged in concentric circles and are linked together by four (shaded) portions of the figure that emphasize that the school's accomplishments have the desired effect only when students, teachers, and parents actively choose to commit effort in ways that support student learning.

Four accomplishments—the learning goals the school defines, the instruction it provides, the climate it creates for students, and the related services it provides to help students benefit from instruction—create the school's environment for learning. By meeting these accomplishments at a high level, schools create conditions that support student effort and focus that effort on academic work that results in learning.

Four additional accomplishments create the environment for teaching and support the effort that school staff spend on their work. The school's creativity in seeking resources; its support for daily operations through schedules, assignments, and so on; its support for staff; and its processes for renewal and change all affect the kind of environment in which teachers work, ultimately affecting what students learn.

The ninth accomplishment, the school's partnership with its families and communities, affects both the environment for learning and the environment for teaching. When that partnership encourages parents to support student effort at home, the impact of the learning environment is magnified. And when that partnership encourages parent involvement in the school, the environment for teaching is enhanced with volunteer support, additional resources, and consistent expectations for behavior in the home and school.

The open space to the right of the figure represents the many factors that influence student learning that are outside the school's control, while the space to left of the figure could have been filled with the institutional context within which schools work—their districts, state agencies, courts, and so on. While noting the importance of both sets of influences, the Framework focuses specifically on issues within a single school.

To help readers use this model to organize their planning and thinking about school leadership, the following sections describe each part of the Framework, beginning at the center with a focus on student learning.

Student Learning

Learning is change over time in behavior, skills, knowledge, or dispositions that occurs as a result of individual attention and effort. Learning is an individual accomplishment—no one can do the learning for someone else.

Learning is the center of the Framework because it is the outcome that everyone—parents, taxpayers, politicians, teachers, and so on—expects from schools. There are other expectations, of course, including scheduled supervision of children, sports events, entertainment, nutrition, and health screening, but student learning provides the essential starting point for an analysis of school work.

This ready agreement about the central importance of learning masks an intense debate about whose learning is important, what should be learned, and how the learning should be assessed. For example, is it more important for students to learn specific facts and values associated with traditional American culture, or for them to develop critical thinking skills that might prompt questions about that culture? Is it important to learn the literature and history of many cultures and religions, or to explore our own heritage more deeply? Should the students learn skills needed for work or those expected for college entry? Although content standards and state tests have forged a partial answer to these questions, local differences remain, and different priorities within school communities can lead to significant conflicts.

As a practical matter, however, each school must use measures of student learning as the focal point for both its internal work and its communication with the community.

Internally, measures of individual student learning provide ongoing feedback about the success of various methods, units, and programs. Using this feedback, successful schools continually solve common school problems in ways that promote student learning and refine their solutions so that more and more learning occurs.

Externally, measures of student learning are central to the school's communication with its community. School and community leaders select assessments that show the overall progress made by students in a school or district and use these tests to demonstrate success in promoting student learning.

The Environment for Learning

The first tier of accomplishments in the figure shapes the school's environment for learning and includes the accomplishments that have the most direct influence on students and their learning. Of course, student learning is most immediately influenced by students' own effort, so this is directly adjacent to student learning in the figure.

Schools influence student effort and learning directly through four of the accomplishments clustered in the first tier of the figure—the nature of the learning goals that are defined, the quality of the instruction that is provided, the climate that is sustained for students, and the related services that are provided. The fifth accomplishment in the learning environment—the nature of the school's partnership with families and the community—affects student learning indirectly, through the support that students receive from their families and communities. These five accomplishments frame the most immediate challenges for a school and its principal to focus on student learning.

Student Effort

Student effort is the process of learning. It involves showing up, remembering needed materials, paying attention, completing work, committing time to school activities, attending class, trying hard, and selecting difficult courses. Most current measures of student effort rely on student responses to questionnaires, although other measures, such as attendance, tardiness, homework completion rates, and discipline referrals, also fit our definition of student effort.

Schools depend on student effort to reach their goals for learning but compete with many outside influences. For example, student effort is affected by parenting strategies, peer group membership, and extent of employment (Steinberg, 1996). Despite these influences, schools can and do support student effort through the quality of the five accomplishments that form the environment for learning in the figure. The success criteria for each of these accomplishments include factors that influence the level and focus of student effort.

Learning Goals Defined

What are learning goals? From an accomplishment perspective, learning goals are the formal statements used by a school to describe what students are expected to learn. As such, they constitute the school's intended curriculum. We use the term *learning goals* to encompass content standards, exit outcomes, and graduation requirements and to refer to the knowledge that students are expected to demonstrate. Our concept of learning goals also includes intermediate goals that lead toward these longer-term expectations, so conceptions of sequencing within subjects and alignment across subjects are related to this accomplishment. Although learning goals are increasingly affected by political decisions about content standards and state tests, schools typically do have discretion over many parts of the curriculum, and the goals and actions of professional staff have much to do with the curriculum that is actually delivered.

Why are learning goals important? Although the intended curriculum is never exactly what is delivered in classrooms or learned by students, it nevertheless gives clarity and focus to the school's work. A clear statement of learning goals can reduce teachers' uncertainty about what is expected, guide assessments of student learning, and provide a framework for keeping track of student progress.

Clear learning goals also help to motivate student effort. When students believe that what they are expected to learn relates to their own experiences and aspirations, they are more likely to work hard and learn. Learning goals also affect how much students learn. When more is expected or required in the curriculum, most students learn more.

What success criteria apply to learning goals? Success criteria for the learning goals accomplishment focus on the nature of the goals themselves—What distinguishes good goals for student learning? As a starting point for defining locally useful success criteria, we suggest that high-quality learning goals are:

♦ Ambitious

♦ Comprehensive in relation to state tests

♦ Clearly stated and easily understood

Instruction Provided

What is instruction? Instruction is generally viewed as the interaction among teachers, students, and subject matter through which students are expected to develop new knowledge and skills. To define instruction as an accomplishment involves specifying the results that are expected from these interactions rather than the associated behaviors and processes. From this perspective, we define instruction as *the tasks or assignments expected of students, together with the social and physical context supporting task completion.* Instruction always involves some expectation for student work, even if this is simply a matter of paying attention and remembering (Doyle, 1992; Schlechty, 1990). In addition, these work expectations always occur in a context of support—from the teacher and setting—that can facilitate performance and learning.

Why is instruction important? Instruction is the creative core of a school's work. It determines the work students are expected to do, the activities, assignments, and experiences through which students are expected to reach the school's learning goals. Instruction affects what students learn by the kind of activities that are designed. Teachers rely on assessment of student learning—their own and those provided by formal testing—to make sure that students are assigned work that is challenging but achievable with effort.

Instruction also affects the student's motivation to work and learn by the kind of activities that are selected and the atmosphere of the classroom. By connecting activities to students' experiences and giving quick feedback on student work, teachers increase student effort and learning.

What success criteria apply to instruction? As a starting point for developing locally useful success criteria, we suggest that quality instruction is:

- ◆ Organized to maximize learning time
- ◆ Challenging so that all students can succeed with effort
- ◆ Adapted to learning needs of individual students
- ◆ Feedback-rich so that students know how well they are doing
- ◆ Contextualized so that it is connected to students' prior learning

Student Climate Sustained

What is student climate? We define student climate from an accomplishment perspective as the sum of the school's implicit messages to students about what is important as these are perceived and understood by individual students. Although consistent with the many views of climate and culture as the personality, feel, tone, atmosphere, character, and mood of the school, this definition focuses on the impact on individual students. Our definition emphasizes that the impact of the climate on student effort and learning depends on each student's perception and interpretation of the school's messages and acknowledges that these messages can come from the school as a whole, the classroom, or any other subgroup in the school.

Why is student climate important? Students' perceptions of the school's climate seem to affect their satisfaction, effort, attendance, dropout rates, and, ultimately, their learning. Although different aspects of climate are important to different students and groups, some of the school's implicit messages probably are important to everyone.

What success criteria apply to the student climate accomplishment? As a starting point for developing local success criteria, we suggest that when a high-quality climate exists, students believe that the school

- ◆ Emphasizes academic learning
- ◆ Is safe and orderly
- ◆ Promotes strong, healthy relationships with peers and adults

Related Services Provided

What are related services? From an accomplishment perspective, we define related services as *the supports provided to students that help them benefit from instruction and other school programs.* Schools provide many of these services. The term "related services" comes from special education legislation, where it includes transportation to and from school, school health services, speech and language therapy, physical and occupational therapies, counseling and psychological services, social work services, therapeutic recreation, and assistive technology services. Because schools provide many of these and other services to other students as well, we take an even broader view. In addition to the traditional special education services, our more inclusive definition includes school breakfast and lunch programs, college preparation advising, special programs to reduce use of illegal drugs, and so on.

Why are related services important? Although sometimes criticized as requirements for schools to attend to factors outside their primary responsibility for teaching and learning, related services can be essential for many students to reach learning goals. Students come to school with very different needs, but they all are expected to reach expected standards for learning. Related services help schools address some of these differences in ways that make instruction more effective.

What success criteria apply to related services? As a starting point for defining locally useful success criteria, we suggest that high-quality related services are:

♦ Focused on and responsive to learning problems

♦ Based on thorough assessments that demonstrate need

The Environment for Teaching

The quality of the school's environment for learning depends on the effort of the school's staff. Consistently striving for excellence in the learning environment for all students requires extraordinary commitment. Schools and their principals provide direct support for professional effort through four accomplishments that are clustered in the second tier of the figure. Schools (1) obtain resources to support their operations, (2) allocate those resources to support daily operations, (3) create a culture for the staff, and (4) establish processes for organizational change and renewal. The fifth accomplishment, the school–family–school partnership, influences professional effort indirectly, when parents choose to become involved in the school. The quality with which each of these accomplishments is realized affects the level and focus of professional effort, in turn affecting the school's environment for learning and, ultimately, student effort and learning.

Professional Effort

Like most organizations, schools depend on the motivation and skills of their employees to do the work necessary to achieve goals. The amount of staff effort, and its direction and persistence, have much to do with whether organizations succeed or fail. And, because teaching is such complex work, professional effort in schools is particularly important. The difference between particularly successful schools and others is often the extraordinary effort that teachers commit to the tasks of instruction and relationship building with students and parents.

Resources Mobilized

What is the resources mobilized accomplishment? All schools depend on fiscal, human, and material resources to reach their goals, and school leaders typically must seek these resources from the school district, community, families, and other sources. In order to garner resources that the school can apply to meet its purposes, principals complete budget proposals, recruit volunteers, write grants, request needed services, recruit potential staff, and so on. Of course, the actual resources obtained through this effort often are out of the school's control. Consequently, we define the resources mobilized accomplishment as *the school's external communications regarding needs, plans, programs, and resources.*

This definition includes a wide range of communications associated with seeking fiscal, human, and material resources and services. With the growth of choice plans and charter schools, an increasingly important part of many schools' resource development efforts relates to recruitment of students and parents. Because school funding often depends on the number of students served, enrollment management has become an important part of how a school creates its resource base. Consequently, the resources mobilized accomplishment includes areas such as orienting new parents, direct recruitment activities, school tours, and more general marketing strategies associated with branding and advertising.

Why is mobilizing resources important? The ability to do the work of the school is affected by the amount, type, and timeliness of the resources and supports that are available. Although these traditional input measures are not always directly related to student achievement, they nevertheless help to define the barriers that schools must overcome in meeting their objectives. In addition, staff and students are encouraged to enhance their efforts when they believe that school leadership is doing everything possible to secure needed resources.

What success criteria apply to mobilizing resources? A starting point for development of local success criteria include expectations that efforts to secure resources are:

- Creative in identifying opportunities
- Comprehensive in relation to the school's needs
- Aligned with school goals

School Operations Organized and Supported

What is the school operations accomplishment? To support daily operations with the resources they have, schools use a variety of organizational structures, policies, job assignments, schedules, and plans. We define a school's support for operations as *its allocation of physical, human, fiscal, and information resources to various aspects of the school's work.* This allocation of resources creates the work system of the school, clarifying what is to be done; who will do it; where the work will be located; what equipment, information, and supplies are available to support it; what standards exist for performance; who will evaluate the work; and what help is available. The result that is achieved as a school supports its operations is a pattern of resource allocations, a definition of how the school's human, monetary, physical, and informational resources will be used.

Why are school operations important? Although de-emphasized in some professional literature as involving management rather than leadership, the details of school operations command considerable attention from school administrators and often provide the means through which other leadership goals are achieved. Because school operations result in the schedule, budget, job assignments, and space allocation in the school, they have a pervasive effect on how time and other resources are allocated to various goals for student learning and school improvement.

What success criteria apply to a school's support for operations? As a starting point for defining local success criteria, we suggest that support for operations should:

- Focus resources (time, expertise, facilities) on learning priorities
- Define clear expectations for everyone

Support for Staff

What is included in the staff support accomplishment? We define the accomplishment "staff supported" as the implicit and explicit messages that teachers receive from the principal and school about what is expected, together with the social and administrative support they receive to meet those expectations. Schools and their principals work toward this accomplishment through activities associated with a broad range of human resource functions, including staff supervision, evaluation, and professional development, along with strategies to foster strong cultures, shared values, and high motivation.

Why is staff support important? Schools make long-term investments in teachers and other staff and then depend on these individuals' work as the primary means of reaching school accomplishments and achieving student learning outcomes. The kinds of support that schools provide can affect the skills and commitment of staff and the resulting student learning.

What success criteria apply to the staff support accomplishment? As a starting point for the development of local success criteria, we suggest that staff support is of high quality when professionals in the building feel that they are:

- Known well and respected
- Evaluated fairly
- Given help to do their jobs well
- Given opportunities to continue learning
- Given opportunities to work together

School Renewal Supported

What is the support for school renewal accomplishment? To reach their accomplishments at quality levels that promote learning for all students, schools must constantly adapt to new students, parent expectations, required tests and curricula, technologies, school board policies, and program possibilities. We define the accomplishment "school renewal supported" as *the set of processes and structures that a school has in place to provide itself feedback on its effectiveness, set goals for improvement, support implementation of new procedures, and evaluate results.* Note that the accomplishment is not the actual changes that the school is able to implement; rather, it is the nature of the system that the school has established to define, support, and evaluate those changes.

Why is the school renewal accomplishment important? Change in schools can be as difficult as it is important. Having a clear process for organizational renewal can (a) help ensure that changes in the school respond to priority local problems rather than simply reflecting currently popular programs; (b) help to focus the school's efforts to improve so that faculty, staff, administrators, and volunteers all are attending to the same concerns; (c) help create confidence in the school's decisions by making the decision process clear and well known; and (d) help the school develop better and better strategies for dealing with its problems as everyone becomes comfortable with a process of assessment, goal setting, and implementation.

What success criteria apply to school renewal? As a starting point for development of local success criteria, we suggest that a school renewal process is of high quality when it ensures that:

- Feedback is available for frequent monitoring of the school's programs
- Processes for decision making are clear and well understood
- Goals are supported by a working majority of staff and community

The Family and Community Partnership Sustained

The school's partnership with its families and communities is a part of both the environment for learning and the environment for teaching because it has the potential to influence both student effort and professional effort. Whereas the school's activities supporting families and community members typically are an integrated whole, the things that families and community members choose to do as a result of the school's partnership are different as they support student and professional effort. The figure illustrates this by separating family and community support from family and community involvement.

"Family and community support" refers to the assistance and help that students get outside the school. Children and adolescents spend the vast majority of their time outside of the school, at home and in other community settings, and the influences present in those settings have much to do with students' academic effort and learning.

"Family and community involvement" includes a wide array of activities through which parents and community members support professional effort through their engagement in the school. Involvement can include, for example, volunteering and other activities that add resources to the school, and encouraging and supporting teachers' work.

What is the family and community partnerships accomplishment? To promote both involvement and support, the accomplishment—family and community partnerships sustained—includes a wide range of strategies through which the school shares responsibility for child growth and learning with families and other community groups. Our definition emphasizes the school's role in this partnership by focusing on *all the influences exerted by the school to help parents and other community members help children succeed in school.* Consequently, the partnership includes everything the school does to help parents provide basic services to their children and serve as teachers in the home. It also includes the school's efforts to engage parents as volunteers in the operation of the school, as participants in discussions of school plans, and as involved members in school governance.

Why is the family and community partnership important? Students spend only a small fraction of their time in school. If student effort is to be sufficient to reach ambitious learning goals, schools need allies in supporting student effort. Parents, employers, and other community leaders are important potential allies. In fact, the rewards, encouragement, and sanctions that parents and community members can use to support student effort often are much more powerful than those available to the school.

What success criteria apply to family and community partnerships? As a starting point for developing local success criteria, we suggest that schools best support a family and community partnership when it ensures that:

- Information to parents is accessible, frequent, and specific
- Opportunities to participate are frequent and varied
- Parents perceive respect for their culture, language, and beliefs
- Community connections support rapid support for students needing extra help

For More Information about the Framework for School Leadership Accomplishments

Two resources are available for readers who want to learn more about the *Framework for School Leadership Accomplishments*. The book *Principal Accomplishments, How School Leaders Succeed* (Bellamy, Fulmer, Murphy, & Muth, 2007) provides in-depth discussions of leadership strategies associated with the framework and how these strategies suggest new ways of understanding the principalship. A second essay, "Conceptual Foundations for Principal Leadership" (Bellamy, Fulmer, Murphy, & Muth, 2006), reviews research and scholarship related to each accomplishment in the FSLA.

References and Resources

The references used in this book, along with other resources that will assist beginning principals in continuously improving, appear in this section categorized by each of the nine accomplishment areas of the *Framework of School Leadership Accomplishments* for easy perusal.

Preface

Barth, R. S. (1990). *Improving schools from within: Teachers, parents and principals can make the difference.* San Francisco: Jossey-Bass Publishers.

Larson, J. (composer-lyricist). *Seasons of Love*, song from Broadway musical *Rent*. Finster & Lucy Music Ltd., 1996.

Chapter 1 and Appendix: The Framework for School Leadership Accomplishments

Ballek, K., O'Rourke, A., Provenzano, J., & Bellamy, T. (2005). Seven keys in cultivating principals and teacher leaders. *Journal of Staff Development, 26*(2), 42–29.

Bellamy, T., Fulmer, C., Murphy, M., & Muth, R. (2003). *A framework for school leadership accomplishments: A perspective on knowledge, practice, and preparation for principals. Leadership and Policy in Schools, 2*(4), 241–261.

Bellamy, G. T., Fulmer, C. L., Murphy, M. J., & Muth, R. (2006). Conceptual foundations for principal leadership. In A. Danzig. K. Borman, B. Jones, & W. Wright (Eds.), *Learner-centered leadership: Research, policy, and practice.* Mahwah, NJ: Lawrence Erlbaum.

Bellamy, G. T., Fulmer, C. L., Murphy, M. J., & Muth, R. (2007). *Principal accomplishments: How school leaders succeed.* New York: Teachers College Press.

Bellamy, T. (1999). *The whole school framework: A design for learning.* Oxford, OH: National Staff Development Council.

Doyle, W. (1992). Curriculum and pedagogy. In P. Jackson (Ed.), *Handbook of research on curriculum* (pp. 486–516). New York: Macmillan.

Schlechty, P. (1990). *Schools for the 21st century: Leadership imperatives for educational reform.* San Francisco: Jossey-Bass.

Senge, P. (1990). *The fifth discipline: The art and practice of the learning organization.* New York: Doubleday.

Steinberg, L. (1996). *Beyond the classroom: Why school reform has failed and what parents need to do.* New York: Simon & Schuster.

Chapter 2: Defining Learning Goals

Carr, J. F., & Harris, D. E. (2001). *Succeeding with standards: Linking curriculum, assessment, and action planning.* Alexandria, VA: Association for Supervision and Curriculum Development.

Marzano, R. J. (2003). *What works in schools: Translating research into action.* Alexandria, VA: Association for Supervision and Curriculum Development.

Reeves, D. B. (2002). *The leader's guide to standards: A blueprint for educational equity and excellence.* San Francisco: Jossey-Bass.

Shea, M. R. (2005) *From standards to success.* Alexandria, VA: Association for Supervision and Curriculum Development.

Solomon, P. (1998). *The curriculum bridge: From standards to actual classroom practice.* Thousand Oaks, CA: Corwin Press.

Chapter 3: Providing Instruction

Downey, C. T., Steffy, B. E., English, F. W., Frase, L. E., & Poston, W. K., Jr. (2004). *The three-minute classroom walk-through.* Thousand Oaks, CA: Corwin Press.

Easton, L. B. (2004). *Powerful designs for professional learning.* Oxford, OH: National Staff Development Council.

Marzano, R., & Kendall, J. (1996). *Designing standards-based districts, school s and classrooms.* Alexandria, VA: Association for Supervision and Curriculum Development, McREL.

Marzano, R., Pickering, D., & Pollock, J. (2001). *Classroom instruction that works: Research-based strategies for increasing student achievement.* Alexandria, VA: Association for Supervision and Curriculum Development.

Marzano R. J., Norford, J. S., Paynter, D. E., Pickering, D. J., & Gaddy, B. B. (2001). *A handbook for classroom instruction that works.* Alexandria, VA: Association for Supervision and Curriculum Development.

Peters, T. J., & Austin, N. (1985). *A passion for excellence: The leadership difference.* New York: Random House.

Saphier, J., & Gower, R. (1997). *The skillful teachers: Building your teaching skills.* Carlisle, MA: Research for Better Teaching, Inc.

Chapter 4: Sustaining Student Climate

Deal, T., & Peterson, K. (1999). *Shaping school culture.* San Francisco: Jossey-Bass.

Dwyer, K., Osher, D., & Wanger, C. (1998). *Early warning, timely response: A guide to safe schools.* Washington, DC: U.S. Department of Education.

Grady, M. L. (2004). *The 20 biggest mistakes principals make and how to avoid them.* Thousand Oaks, CA: Corwin Press.

Sagor, R. (2003). *Motivating students and teachers in an era of standards.* Alexandria, VA: Association for Supervision and Curriculum Development.

Chapter 5: Providing Related Services

Conzemius, A., & O'Neill, J. (2002). *The handbook for SMART school teams.* Bloomington, IN: National Educational Service.

Chapter 6: Mobilizing Resources

Conzemius, A., & O'Neil, J. (2001). *Building shared responsibility for student learning.* Alexandria, VA: Association for Supervision and Curriculum Development.

Robbins, P., & Alvy, H. (2004). *The new principal's fieldbook: Strategies for success.* Alexandria, VA: Association for Supervision and Curriculum Development.

Chapter 7: Organizing and Supporting School Operations

Blaydes, J. (2004). *Survival skills for the principalship.* Thousand Oaks, CA: Corwin Press.

Dalheim, M. (Ed.). (1994). *Time strategies.* National Education Association.

Danielson, C. (2002). *Enhancing student achievement: A framework for school improvement.* Alexandria, VA: Association for Supervision and Curriculum Development.

Fournies, F. (1999). *Why employees don't do what they're supposed to do and what to do about it.* New York: McGraw-Hill.

Heller, D. A. (2004). *Teachers wanted, attracting and retaining good teachers.* Alexandria, VA: Association for Supervision and Curriculum Development.

Chapter 8: Supporting Staff

Blasé, J., & Kirby, P. (1992). *Bringing out the best in teachers.* Thousand Oaks, CA: Corwin Press.

Connors, N. A. (2000). *If you don't feed the teachers, they eat the students! Guide to success for administrators and teachers.* Nashville, TN: Incentive Publications.

Danielson, C. (1996). *Enhancing professional practice: A framework for teaching.* Alexandria, VA: Association for Supervision and Curriculum Development.

Darling-Hammond, L. (1997). *Quality teaching: The critical key to learning.* Available from http://www.naesp.org/comm/p0997a.htm

Sagor, R. (1996). *Local control and accountability: How to get it, keep it, and improve school performance.* Thousand Oaks, CA: Corwin Press.

Sanders, W. L. (1998). Value-added assessment. *School Administrator, 55*(11). Available from: http://www.aasa.org/SchoolAdmin/dec9801.htm

Saphier, J. (1993). *How to make supervision & evaluation really work: Supervision and evaluation in the context of strengthening school culture.* Acton, MA: Research for Better Teaching.

Saphier, J., & King, M. (1985). *Good seeds grow in strong cultures. Educational Leadership, 42*(6), 67–84.

Chapter 9: Supporting School Renewal

Bernhardt, V. L. (1998). *Data analysis for comprehensive schoolwide improvement.* Princeton, NJ: Eye On Education.

Conzemius, A., & O'Neill, J. (2002). *The handbook for SMART school teams.* Bloomington, IN: National Educational Service.

Facilitative leadership. (1994). Morrison, CO: Colorado Staff Development Council.

Garmston, R., & Wellman, B. M. (1999). *The adaptive school: A sourcebook for developing collaborative groups.* Norwood, MA: Christopher-Gordon Publishers.

Holcomb, E. L. (1999). *Getting excited about data: How to combine people, passion, and proof.* Thousand Oaks, CA: Corwin Press.

Kaner, S., Lind, L., Toldi, C., Fisk, S., & Berger, D. (1996). *Facilitator's guide to participatory decision-making.* Gabriola Island, BC: New Society Publishers/Canada (Fifteenth Printing, April, 2005).

Reeves, D. (2004). *Accountability for learning: How teachers and school leaders can take charge.* Alexandria, VA: Association for Supervision and Curriculum Development.

Schwarz, R. M. (2002). *The skilled facilitator.* San Francisco: Jossey-Bass.

Chapter 10: Sustaining Family-Community Partnerships

Barth, R. S. (1990). *Improving schools from within: Teachers, parents and principals can make the difference.* San Francisco: Jossey-Bass Publishers.

127 Ideas Principals Can Use Now to Build a Successful Parent Involvement Program. Presentation by John H. Wherry, President, The Parent Institute, Fairfax Station, Virginia, at the 1997 NAESP Convention, San Anotonio, Texas, March 14, 1997.

Pawlas, G. E. (2005). *The administrator's guide to school-community relations* (2nd ed.). Princeton, NJ: Eye On Education.

Rioux, J. W., & Berla, N. (1993). *Innovations in parent and family involvement.* Princeton, NJ: Eye On Education.

Index